Explore Germany's Rich Culture and Sce
Europe Travel Guide - Munich, Berlin, N
and Beyond

CW00556168

Crafted by a 15-Year European Resident, ~~discover~~ ~~the~~ ~~~~
Germany Like a Local!

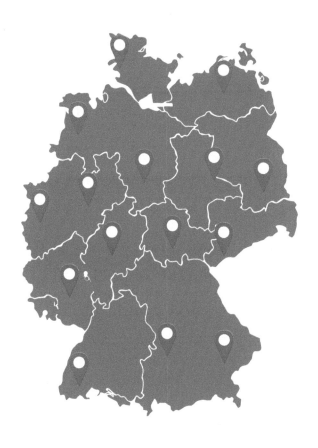

Table Of Contents

Chapter 1: Top 15 Places to Visit in Germany as a Tourist and Why They Are Special

Berlin: A Blend of History and Modernity

Berlin, the capital city of Germany, is a fascinating destination that seamlessly combines a rich historical heritage with a vibrant modern atmosphere. It is a city that has witnessed signi cant events that shaped the course of history, and yet has emerged as a contemporary hub of art, culture, and innovation.

One of the key reasons why Berlin is special is its historical significance. The city has been at the center of major events, from the rise and fall of the Berlin Wall to the reunification of Germany. Visitors can explore iconic landmarks such as the Brandenburg Gate, a symbol of peace and unity, and the remnants of the Berlin Wall, which serves as a poignant reminder of the city's divided past.

In addition to its historical sites, Berlin is a hub for museums that offer a deep dive into Germany's past. The Museum Island, a UNESCO World Heritage Site, houses ve world-class museums, including the Pergamon Museum and the Neues Museum. These institutions showcase artifacts and artworks from various periods, providing visitors with a comprehensive understanding of German history and culture.

However, Berlin is not just a city frozen in time. It is a vibrant metropolis that embraces modernity and innovation. The city is renowned for its thriving art scene, with numerous galleries, street art, and contemporary exhibitions. Visitors can explore the trendy neighborhoods of Kreuzberg and Friedrichshain, which are home to a plethora of art studios, alternative fashion boutiques, and hip cafés.

Berlin is also a melting pot of cultures, with a diverse culinary scene that caters to all tastes. From traditional German cuisine to international flavors, the city offers a wide range of dining options. Visitors can indulge in traditional dishes like sausages and sauerkraut, or explore the vibrant food markets and street food stalls that showcase flavors from around the world.

Moreover, Berlin hosts several cultural festivals throughout the year, attracting visitors from all over the globe. Events like the Berlin International Film Festival and the Carnival of Cultures showcase the city's multiculturalism and artistic prowess.

In conclusion, Berlin is a city that seamlessly blends its historical past with a modern, forward-thinking outlook. It offers visitors a unique opportunity to explore its iconic landmarks, dive into its rich history through museums, experience its vibrant art scene, and indulge in its diverse culinary offerings. Whether you are a history enthusiast, an art lover, or a foodie, Berlin has something to captivate every traveler.

Munich: Bavarian Culture and World-Class Museums

Munich, the capital of Bavaria, is a city that effortlessly combines rich cultural traditions with world-class museums. It is a must-visit destination for any tourist or traveler seeking to immerse themselves in the vibrant German culture. In this subchapter, we will explore the highlights of Munich, from its Bavarian heritage to its renowned museums. Bavarian Culture

Munich is often referred to as the cultural heart of Bavaria, and it's easy to see why. The city's historic center, with its charming cobblestone streets and traditional architecture, exudes a sense of old-world charm. Visitors can explore the iconic Marienplatz, the central square, which is home to the famous Glockenspiel and the stunning New Town Hall. The Viktualienmarkt, a bustling open-air market, offers a taste of Bavarian cuisine, with vendors selling everything from pretzels to sausages. World-Class Museums

Munich is also known for its exceptional museums, which house a wealth of art, history, and science. The Alte Pinakothek, one of the oldest art galleries in the world, showcases masterpieces from renowned artists such as Rembrandt, Rubens, and Dürer. For lovers of modern art, the Pinakothek der Moderne is a must-visit, with its extensive collection of contemporary works. History buffs will appreciate the Munich Documentation Center for the History of National Socialism, which sheds light on Germany's dark past.

A visit to Munich would not be complete without exploring the world-famous Deutsche's Museum. This expansive museum is the largest of its kind in the world and covers a wide range of scientific and technological disciplines. With exhibits on everything from astronomy to aviation, visitors can delve into the fascinating world of science and innovation.

In addition to its cultural and artistic offerings, Munich is also famous for its lively festivals. Oktoberfest, the world's largest beer festival, attracts millions of visitors each year who come to experience the vibrant atmosphere and indulge in traditional Bavarian food and drink. The Christmas markets, with their beautifully decorated stalls selling crafts and delicacies, are a magical sight to behold.

Munich truly embodies the essence of Bavarian culture and offers an unparalleled experience for tourists and travelers. From its charming streets and traditional markets to its world-class museums and lively festivals, the city has something to offer for everyone. A visit to Munich is a journey into the heart of Bavaria's vibrant culture and a chance to explore the best of German history and art.

Cologne: Gothic Architecture and the Rhine River

Cologne, a city located on the banks of the majestic Rhine River, is a treasure trove of Gothic architecture and historical significance. As one of the top 15 places to visit in Germany, Cologne offers a unique blend of old-world charm and modern vibrancy that attracts tourists and travelers from all over the world.

The highlight of Cologne's architectural marvels is the iconic Cologne Cathedral, a UNESCO World Heritage Site. This grand Gothic masterpiece took over six centuries to complete and is considered one of the most impressive cathedrals in the world. Its intricate details, soaring spires, and stunning stained-glass windows will leave you in awe. Climb to the top of the cathedral's tower for panoramic views of the city and the Rhine River.

While exploring the city, make sure to stroll along the banks of the Rhine River, which has been an important trade route for centuries. Take a leisurely boat cruise to admire the picturesque scenery and enjoy the refreshing breeze. The Rheinauhafen district, with its modern architecture and vibrant atmosphere, is a must-visit for its trendy bars, restaurants, and shops.

Cologne is also home to numerous museums that offer insights into its rich history and culture. The Museum Ludwig houses an extensive collection of modern and contemporary art, including works by Picasso and Warhol. The Romano-Germanic Museum showcases Roman artifacts, including the famous Dionysus mosaic. History buffs will also appreciate the Chocolate Museum, where you can learn about the history of chocolate and indulge in some delicious treats.

For a taste of Cologne's vibrant culture, visit during the annual Cologne Carnival, one of the largest street festivals in Europe. Join the locals in colorful costumes, dance to lively music, and immerse yourself in the festive atmosphere.

With its captivating Gothic architecture, picturesque Rhine River views, and vibrant cultural scene, Cologne is a must-visit destination for any traveler exploring Germany's historical cities. Whether you are an architecture enthusiast, history lover, or simply seeking a unique cultural experience, Cologne has something to offer to everyone. So, make sure to include this enchanting city in your itinerary and create memories that will last a lifetime.

Hamburg: Maritime Charm and Speicherstadt Warehouse District

As you embark on your journey to discover Germany's industrial heritage, make sure to include a visit to Hamburg, a city that exudes maritime charm and boasts the iconic Speicherstadt Warehouse District. Located in northern Germany, Hamburg is not only the country's second-largest city but also one of its most vibrant and historically significant destinations.

The maritime charm of Hamburg is evident as soon as you arrive in the city. With its bustling port, picturesque waterfront, and numerous canals, Hamburg has a strong connection to the sea. Take a stroll along the Elbe River and witness the comings and goings of ships from all over the world or hop on a boat tour to explore the city's waterways and experience its maritime heritage Firsthand.

One of the highlights of Hamburg is the Speicherstadt Warehouse District, a UNESCO World Heritage Site. This historic district is a testament to Germany's industrial past and offers a unique insight into the country's trading history. Built in the late 19th century, the red-brick warehouses were once used to store goods such as spices, coffee, and carpets. Today, they have been transformed into a vibrant cultural and commercial hub, housing museums, galleries, shops, and even a chocolate factory.

Wandering through the narrow streets and canals of Speicherstadt, you'll be transported back in time. Admire the impressive architecture, with its intricate façades, gabled roofs, and ornamental details. Step inside the museums and learn about Hamburg's maritime history, or explore the vibrant art scene that has flourished within the district. Don't forget to stop by the Miniature Wonderland, the world's largest model railway exhibition, located in the heart of Speicherstadt.

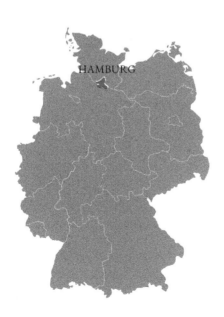

Beyond the Speicherstadt Warehouse District, Hamburg has much more to offer. Explore the vibrant neighborhoods of St. Pauli and Sternschanze, known for their lively nightlife, trendy bars, and unique boutiques. Visit the historic St. Michael's Church, known as the "Michel," and climb to the top for panoramic views of the city. Immerse yourself in the local culture by attending a performance at the Elbphilharmonie, one of the most acoustically advanced concert halls in the world.

For a taste of Hamburg's culinary delights, head to the Fischmarkt, where you can indulge in freshly caught seafood or sample local delicacies like Labskaus, a traditional sailor's dish. And if you're looking for some relaxation, take a leisurely walk in the beautiful Planten un Blomen park or enjoy a boat ride on the Alster Lake.

Hamburg is a city that seamlessly blends its industrial heritage with modern attractions, making it a must-visit destination for any traveler seeking a unique and enriching experience. So, pack your bags and get ready to explore the maritime charm and history of this remarkable city.

Frankfurt: Skyscrapers and Cultural Diversity

As you explore the top 15 places to visit in Germany, one city that should not be missed is Frankfurt. Known for its impressive skyline and cultural diversity, Frankfurt offers a unique blend of modernity and tradition.

When it comes to skyscrapers, Frankfurt is a city that stands out. As the nancial capital of Germany, it boasts one of the most impressive skylines in Europe. The city is home to the iconic Commerzbank Tower, the Messeturm, and the Main Tower, which offers panoramic views of the city from its observation deck. Walking through the city streets, you'll be amazed by the towering glass facades and modern architectural marvels that dominate the landscape.

But Frankfurt is not just about skyscrapers. The city is also a melting pot of cultures, making it a vibrant and diverse destination. With over 180 nationalities represented, Frankfurt is a true cosmopolitan city. It is home to a thriving arts scene, with numerous galleries and museums showcasing works from around the world. The Städel Museum, for example, houses an impressive collection of European art, while the Museum of Applied Arts showcases contemporary design and craftsmanship.

In addition to its cultural offerings, Frankfurt also hosts a number of festivals and events throughout the year. The Frankfurt Book Fair, one of the largest book fairs in the world, attracts visitors from all over the globe. The Museumsuferfest, a three-day festival held along the banks of the River Main, celebrates the city's cultural heritage with live music, art exhibitions, and culinary delights.

If you're a food lover, Frankfurt will not disappoint. The city is known for its diverse culinary scene, offering everything from traditional German cuisine to international flavors. Don't miss the opportunity to try local specialties such as "Frankfurter Grüne Sauce" (green sauce) or "Ebbelwoi" (apple wine) in one of the traditional apple wine taverns.

Frankfurt's central location also makes it an ideal starting point for exploring other parts of Germany. With excellent transportation connections, you can easily visit nearby cities such as Heidelberg, Wiesbaden, or the picturesque Rhine Valley.

In conclusion, Frankfurt is a city of contrasts, where towering skyscrapers coexist with rich cultural diversity. Whether you're fascinated by modern architecture or eager to immerse yourself in different cultures, Frankfurt has something to offer every traveler.

Rothenburg ob der Tauber: Step into a Fairytale Village

Nestled in the heart of Bavaria, the picturesque village of Rothenburg ob der Tauber is a true gem that will transport you to a fairytale world. This enchanting destination has captivated tourists and travelers alike with its half- timbered houses, cobblestone streets, and preserved medieval architecture. Rothenburg ob der Tauber is not just a place to visit; it is an experience that will leave you spellbound.

As you step into Rothenburg ob der Tauber, you will be transported back in time to the Middle Ages. The village's well-preserved city walls, dating back to the 14th century, offer a glimpse into its rich history and provide breathtaking views of the surrounding countryside. Walking along the cobbled streets, you will encounter charming shops selling handmade crafts, traditional bakeries offering mouth-watering pastries, and cozy cafes where you can savor a cup of hot chocolate.

One of the highlights of Rothenburg ob der Tauber is the famous Plönlein, a picturesque square adorned with colorful half-timbered houses. This iconic spot has been featured in numerous postcards and is the perfect backdrop for an unforgettable photo. From Plönlein, you can wander through the narrow streets and admire the stunning architecture of the town hall, the St. James Church, and the medieval Criminal Museum, which offers a fascinating insight into the justice system of the past.

Rothenburg ob der Tauber is also known for its annual Christmas market, which transforms the village into a winter wonderland. The market, held from late November to late December, features stalls selling handmade crafts, delicious local delicacies, and festive decorations. Visitors can immerse themselves in the magical atmosphere, listen to carol singers, and warm up with a cup of mulled wine.

For those seeking a more immersive experience, the Night Watchman's Tour is a must-do. Led by a costumed guide, this evening tour takes you through the darkened streets of Rothenburg ob der Tauber, sharing stories and legends from the village's past. As you walk in the footsteps of the night watchman, you will gain a deeper understanding of the history and culture of this fairytale village.

Rothenburg ob der Tauber is a truly special place that offers a unique glimpse into Germany's rich history and medieval charm. Whether you are a history enthusiast, a lover of fairy tales, or simply seeking a magical escape, this village should be at the top of your list when visiting Germany. Step into Rothenburg ob der Tauber and let the enchantment of this fairytale village sweep you away.

Heidelberg: Romanticism and the Famous Heidelberg Castle

When it comes to fairytale-like castles, Heidelberg Castle is a must-visit destination in Germany. Situated in the charming city of Heidelberg, this castle holds a significant place in the country's history and offers a romantic experience for tourists and travelers alike.

Heidelberg Castle, perched on a hill overlooking the city, is a testament to the romanticism and grandeur of the past. Its origins can be traced back to the 13th century, and over the years, it has evolved into an architectural masterpiece. The castle complex encompasses various structures, including the Friedrich Building, the Ottheinrich Building, and the iconic Great Barrel, which holds the Guinness World Record as the largest wine barrel in the world.

As you explore the castle's grounds, you'll be captivated by its enchanting gardens, terraces, and courtyards. The stunning views of the Neckar River and the surrounding forests add to the castle's allure, making it an ideal spot for capturing breathtaking photographs and creating lasting memories.

Inside the castle, you can delve into its rich history through the Heidelberg Castle Museum. Discover artifacts, paintings, and historical exhibitions that provide insights into the castle's signi cance as a cultural and political hub in the past. Be sure to also visit the famous Pharmacy Museum, which showcases an extensive collection of pharmaceutical tools, medicines, and equipment from centuries ago.

To make your visit truly memorable, consider attending one of the many cultural events hosted at Heidelberg Castle. From open-air concerts to theater performances, these events bring the castle to life and offer a unique way to experience its splendor.

Beyond the castle, Heidelberg itself is a romantic city with a vibrant atmosphere. Take a stroll along the picturesque streets of the Old Town, visit the renowned Heidelberg University, or enjoy a boat ride on the Neckar River. The city also boasts a lively dining scene, where you can savor traditional German cuisine and world-class wines.

Heidelberg, with its romantic castle and charming surroundings, is undoubtedly one of the top places to visit in Germany. Whether you're a history enthusiast, a lover of architecture, or simply seeking a romantic getaway, this destination promises an unforgettable experience that will leave you enchanted by its beauty and allure.

Neuschwanstein Castle: A Fairy Tale Come to Life

Nestled among the picturesque landscapes of Bavaria, Germany, stands a castle so enchanting, it seems to have sprung from the pages of a fairy tale. Neuschwanstein Castle, also known as the "Cinderella Castle," is a true testament to the romanticism and opulence of the 19th century. This architectural masterpiece has captured the imagination of millions, serving as the inspiration for Disney's Sleeping Beauty castle and captivating visitors from around the world.

Built by King Ludwig II of Bavaria in the late 19th century, Neuschwanstein Castle was intended as a private retreat for the reclusive king. Its exterior, with its towering turrets and whimsical spires, evokes a sense of wonder and awe. As you approach the castle, you can't help but be transported back in time to an era of knights, princesses, and magical adventures.

Stepping inside Neuschwanstein Castle is like entering a fairy tale world. The interior is adorned with intricate woodcarvings, elaborate murals, and lavish furnishings, all meticulously designed to reflect the romantic ideals of the king. The highlight of the castle is undoubtedly the breathtaking Throne Room, a grand space adorned with golden hues and intricate mosaics, fit for a king.

But Neuschwanstein Castle is not the only fairy tale-like castle Germany has to offer. Throughout the country, you will find a multitude of castles, each with its own unique story and charm. Heidelberg Castle, perched high above the city, offers stunning views of the Neckar River and is steeped in history. Hohenzollern Castle, located on a

hilltop, in the Swabian Alps, is a picture-perfect fortress that seems to have leapt straight out of a storybook.

For those who seek a truly magical experience, Germany's fairy tale castles are a must-visit. These architectural wonders transport you to a world of knights and princesses, where dreams come true and happily ever afters are just within reach. Whether you are a history enthusiast, a lover of art and architecture, or simply someone who wants to experience the magic of a fairy tale, Neuschwanstein Castle and its counterparts across Germany will leave you spellbound.

Hohenzollern Castle: Majestic Views and Royal History

Perched atop a hill in the Swabian Alps, Hohenzollern Castle stands as a testament to Germany's rich royal history and offers visitors breathtaking views of the surrounding countryside. This fairy tale-like castle is a must-visit destination for tourists and travelers looking to immerse themselves in the charm of Germany's historical landmarks.

As one of Germany's most iconic fairy tale castles, Hohenzollern Castle captures the imagination with its stunning architecture and picturesque setting. Built in the 19th century, the castle boasts a blend of Gothic Revival and Neo-Gothic styles, creating a truly magni cent sight that has captivated visitors for centuries. Its towers, turrets, and battlements evoke a sense of grandeur and romance, transporting visitors back to a time of knights and princesses.

Stepping inside Hohenzollern Castle, visitors are greeted by opulent interiors adorned with intricate woodwork, exquisite tapestries, and priceless works of art. The castle's museum offers a fascinating glimpse into the lives of the Hohenzollern dynasty, one of Germany's most influential noble families. From royal portraits to ancient artifacts, the museum's collection showcases the wealth and power of the Hohenzollerns throughout history.

Beyond its architectural and historical significance, Hohenzollern Castle offers panoramic views of the rolling hills and lush forests that surround it. Visitors can hike up to the castle or take a shuttle bus to the entrance, enjoying the scenic beauty of the Swabian Alps along the way. Once at the top, they are rewarded with sweeping vistas that stretch as far as the eye can see, providing the perfect backdrop for memorable photographs.

For those seeking a deeper understanding of Germany's royal heritage and a chance to experience the splendor of a bygone era, Hohenzollern Castle is a must-visit attraction. Its majestic views, rich history, and fairy tale-like charm make it a top destination for tourists and travelers exploring Germany's industrial heritage.

So, whether you're a history buff, a lover of architectural marvels, or simply in search of a picturesque destination, Hohenzollern Castle offers a truly unforgettable experience. It is one of the top 15 places to visit in Germany, and its combination of royal history and majestic views make it a special destination that should not be missed.

Mosel Valley: Vineyards and Scenic River Views

The Mosel Valley is a hidden gem in Germany, offering a unique blend of natural beauty and a rich wine culture. Nestled along the banks of the Mosel River, this picturesque region is a must-visit destination for any tourist or traveler seeking a truly enchanting experience.

The Mosel Valley is renowned for its vineyards, which produce some of Germany's finest wines. As you explore the region, you will be greeted by endless rows of lush green vines, stretching as far as the eye can see. The steep slopes of the valley create the perfect conditions for growing grapes, resulting in exceptional wines that are cherished worldwide.

One of the highlights of visiting the Mosel Valley is the opportunity to take part in wine tastings and tours. Many wineries open their doors to visitors, allowing them to sample a variety of wines and learn about the winemaking process. From crisp Rieslings to velvety Pinot Noirs, the Mosel Valley offers a wide range of flavors to satisfy every palate.

In addition to its vineyards, the Mosel Valley boasts breathtaking scenic views. The winding Mosel River is flanked by rolling hills covered in vineyards, creating a postcard-perfect landscape at every turn. Whether you choose to explore the region by foot, bike, or boat, you will be treated to stunning vistas that will leave you in awe.

For those seeking an active adventure, the Mosel Valley offers plenty of hiking and cycling trails. The Moselsteig trail, for example, takes you through charming villages, verdant vineyards, and ancient castles, providing a truly immersive experience in the region's natural beauty.

To truly immerse yourself in the charm of the Mosel Valley, consider staying in one of the many quaint villages that dot the region. Cochem, with its half-timbered houses and medieval castle, is a popular choice for visitors looking to experience the region's romantic atmosphere. Bernkastel-Kues, known for its well-preserved old town and vibrant wine festivals, is another must-visit destination.

In conclusion, the Mosel Valley is a hidden treasure in Germany, offering a perfect blend of vineyards, scenic river views, and charming villages. Whether you are a wine enthusiast, a nature lover, or simply seeking a peaceful retreat, this region has something to offer for everyone. So, make sure to include the Mosel Valley in your itinerary and discover the beauty and flavors that make this place truly special.

Rheingau: Wine Festivals and Picturesque Landscapes

The Rheingau region in Germany offers a magical combination of wine festivals and picturesque landscapes, making it a must-visit destination for wine enthusiasts and nature lovers alike. Located along the banks of the Rhine River, this region is known for its vineyards, wine festivals, and stunning views that will leave you in awe.

One of the highlights of the Rheingau region is its renowned wine culture. The vineyards here produce some of the finest Rieslings in the world, and wine enthusiasts will be delighted to explore the numerous wineries and wine estates that dot the landscape. Take a leisurely stroll through the vineyards, learn about the winemaking process, and indulge in wine tastings to truly appreciate the rich flavors and aromas of the region.

But it's not just about the wine in Rheingau. The region is also blessed with breathtaking natural beauty. The rolling hills covered in vineyards, the charming villages with their half-timbered houses, and the mighty Rhine River winding its way through the landscape create a picturesque setting that is straight out of a postcard. Whether you're exploring the vineyards on foot or taking a scenic boat ride along the Rhine, you'll be treated to stunning views at every turn.

To experience the vibrant wine culture and natural beauty of Rheingau, plan your visit around one of the region's many wine festivals. These festivals are a celebration of the local wine culture and offer a unique opportunity to taste a wide variety of wines, enjoy live music and entertainment, and immerse yourself in the jovial atmosphere. The Rheingau Wine Festival in Wiesbaden and the Rheingau Wine Market in Rüdesheim are just a few of the popular festivals that attract both locals and tourists alike.

In addition to wine festivals, there are plenty of other activities to keep you entertained in Rheingau. Explore the historic towns and castles that are scattered throughout the region, take a relaxing boat ride along the Rhine, or embark on a hike through the vineyards for panoramic views of the surrounding landscape.

Whether you're a wine enthusiast, a nature lover, or simply looking for a charming destination to explore, the Rheingau region in Germany offers a unique blend of wine festivals and picturesque landscapes that will leave you with unforgettable memories. So raise a glass of Riesling, soak in the beauty of the vineyards, and immerse yourself in the vibrant wine culture of Rheingau.

Garmisch-Partenkirchen: Alpine Beauty and Outdoor Adventures

Nestled in the heart of the Bavarian Alps, Garmisch-Partenkirchen is a picturesque town that offers both breathtaking natural beauty and thrilling outdoor adventures. As one of the top 15 places to visit in Germany, this alpine retreat is a must-see for any tourist or traveler seeking an unforgettable experience.

With its snow-capped peaks, lush valleys, and crystal- clear lakes, Garmisch-Partenkirchen is a paradise for nature lovers. From hiking along the famous Partnach Gorge to exploring the breathtaking Zugspitze, Germany's highest mountain, the opportunities for outdoor exploration are endless. Adventurous souls can also try their hand at rock climbing, mountain biking, or paragliding, all while taking in the stunning mountain vistas.

For those seeking a more relaxed experience, Garmisch-Partenkirchen offers plenty of opportunities to unwind and soak in the natural beauty. Take a leisurely stroll through the charming streets of Partenkirchen, with its traditional Bavarian architecture and quaint cafes. Or, indulge in a spa retreat and pamper yourself with thermal baths and wellness treatments in one of the town's renowned spa resorts.

Garmisch-Partenkirchen is not only a haven for outdoor enthusiasts but also a gateway to cultural experiences. Immerse yourself in Bavarian traditions by attending the annual Oktoberfest in Munich, just a short train ride away. Or, visit during the Christmas season and experience the magic of the Nuremberg Christmas markets. The town itself also hosts a variety of cultural events throughout the year, showcasing local music, dance, and art.

With its proximity to the Austrian border, Garmisch-Partenkirchen also offers the opportunity to explore two countries in one trip. Take a day trip to nearby Innsbruck and discover its rich history and stunning architecture, or venture further into Austria's Tyrol region for even more alpine adventures.

Whether you're seeking natural beauty, outdoor thrills, or cultural immersion, Garmisch-Partenkirchen has something for everyone. Its idyllic charm, stunning alpine landscapes, and proximity to other top attractions make it a must-visit destination in Germany. So pack your hiking boots, grab your camera, and get ready to embark on an unforgettable adventure in this alpine paradise.

Berchtesgaden: Stunning Mountain Vistas and Historical Significance

Located in the heart of the Bavarian Alps, Berchtesgaden is a hidden gem that offers both breathtaking natural beauty and a rich historical significance. This picturesque alpine retreat is a must-visit destination for tourists and travelers seeking stunning mountain vistas and a glimpse into Germany's past.

One of the highlights of Berchtesgaden is its majestic mountain landscapes. Nestled in the Watzmann massif, the tallest peak in Germany outside of the Alps, the area offers unparalleled opportunities for hiking, skiing, and enjoying panoramic views. Whether you're an avid outdoor enthusiast or simply looking to relax amidst nature's splendor, Berchtesgaden will not disappoint.

But Berchtesgaden is not just about its natural beauty; it also has a fascinating historical background. During World War II, the area served as Adolf Hitler's mountaintop retreat. Known as the Eagle's Nest, it was a place where Hitler entertained foreign dignitaries and made critical decisions. Today, visitors can explore the Eagle's Nest and learn about this dark chapter in history while taking in the stunning views that once captivated the dictator.

Aside from the Eagle's Nest, Berchtesgaden is also home to the Documentation Center, which provides a comprehensive account of the Nazi era and its impact on the region. This museum offers a thought-provoking insight into Germany's past and serves as a reminder of the importance of learning from history.

In addition to its historical significance, Berchtesgaden also offers a charming town center with traditional Bavarian architecture, quaint shops, and cozy cafes. Strolling through the cobblestone streets, visitors can immerse themselves in the local culture and savor the unique atmosphere of this alpine retreat.

For those seeking a truly unforgettable experience, a visit to Berchtesgaden National Park is a must. This protected area is home to pristine lakes, lush forests, and rare alpine flora and fauna. Exploring the park's hiking trails or taking a boat ride on Lake Königssee will undoubtedly leave visitors in awe of the natural wonders that abound.

In conclusion, Berchtesgaden is a top destination for tourists and travelers seeking stunning mountain vistas and historical significance. Whether you're a nature lover, a history buff, or simply looking for a peaceful retreat, this alpine gem has something to offer everyone. From its breathtaking landscapes to its intriguing historical sites, Berchtesgaden will leave a lasting impression on all who visit.

Oktoberfest in Munich: Celebrating Bavarian Traditions

One of the most iconic and beloved festivals in Germany, Oktoberfest in Munich is a must-visit for any tourist or traveler seeking an authentic Bavarian experience. This subchapter will delve into the rich history and traditions of Oktoberfest, providing insights into why it is a special event that should not be missed.

Oktoberfest is a two-week-long celebration of Bavarian culture, held annually from late September to the rst weekend in October. It originated in 1810 as a royal wedding celebration, but over the years, it has transformed into a grand spectacle that attracts millions of visitors from around the world.

The festival takes place on the Theresienwiese, a large open space in Munich, and features a multitude of attractions and activities. One of the main highlights is the beer tents, where visitors can indulge in the nest Bavarian brews, served in traditional one-liter steins. These tents are operated by different breweries, each with its unique atmosphere and live music performances, creating a lively and jovial ambiance.

Beyond the beer, Oktoberfest offers a wide range of traditional Bavarian cuisine, such as pretzels, sausages, roast chicken, and sauerkraut. Visitors can also enjoy various fairground rides, games, and entertainment options, ensuring there is something for everyone to enjoy.

In addition to the festivities on the Theresienwiese, Oktoberfest is also an opportunity to witness and participate in Bavarian traditions. The opening parade, featuring horse-drawn beer wagons, beautifully dressed locals, and brass bands, sets the tone for the festivities. Visitors can also witness traditional costume fashion shows, dance performances, and even try their hand at Bavarian folk dances.

Oktoberfest is not just a festival; it is an immersion into the heart and soul of Bavaria. It showcases the region's rich cultural heritage, emphasizing the importance of community, tradition, and celebration. Whether you are a beer enthusiast, a lover of Bavarian cuisine, or simply seeking an unforgettable cultural experience, Oktoberfest is an event that will leave a lasting impression.

So, join the millions of visitors who flock to Munich each year and raise your stein in celebration at Oktoberfest. Experience the vibrant atmosphere, the warm hospitality of the locals, and the joyous spirit that permeates every corner of this incredible festival. Prost!

Nuremberg Christmas Markets: A Magical Winter Wonderland

One of the most enchanting experiences you can have while visiting Germany during winter is a trip to the Nuremberg Christmas Markets. These markets transform the city into a magical winter wonderland, offering a unique blend of tradition, holiday cheer, and festive charm.

The Nuremberg Christmas Markets date back to the mid-16th century, making them one of the oldest and most renowned Christmas markets in the country. Each year, the city's main square, known as the Hauptmarkt, is adorned with beautifully decorated wooden stalls,
twinkling lights, and the scent of gingerbread and mulled wine wafting through the air.

As you stroll through the market, you'll discover a wide variety of traditional crafts, handmade gifts, and delicious treats. From intricately carved wooden ornaments and nutcrackers to delicate glass baubles and intricately woven textiles, there's something for everyone on your holiday shopping list. And don't forget to sample the famous Nuremberg gingerbread, known as Lebkuchen, and warm up with a steaming cup of Glühwein (mulled wine).

But the Nuremberg Christmas Markets offer more than just shopping and indulging in culinary delights. The market also features a range of live entertainment, including carol singers, choirs, and musicians, adding to the festive atmosphere. Children will delight in the carousel rides, the chance to meet Santa Claus, and the magical Kinderweihnacht (Children's Christmas) area, with its own small Ferris wheel and merry-go-round.

Beyond the market, the city of Nuremberg itself is steeped in history and offers plenty to explore. Visit the impressive Nuremberg Castle, stroll through the picturesque Old Town, or learn about the city's dark past at the Documentation Center, Nazi Party Rally Grounds.

The Nuremberg Christmas Markets truly capture the essence of the holiday season, making it a must-visit destination for any tourist or traveler exploring Germany. The combination of centuries-old tradition, festive decorations, and warm hospitality creates an unforgettable experience that will leave you with lasting memories. So, bundle up, sip on a cup of Glühwein, and immerse yourself in the magical winter wonderland that is the Nuremberg Christmas Markets.

Chapter 2: Historical Cities: Explore the Rich History of Germany by Visiting Cities like Berlin, Munich, and Cologne

Berlin: From the Brandenburg Gate to the Berlin Wall

Berlin, the vibrant capital of Germany, is a city steeped in history and culture. From the iconic Brandenburg Gate to the haunting Berlin Wall, this subchapter explores the must-see landmarks and historical sites that make Berlin a top destination for tourists and travelers.

The Brandenburg Gate stands as a symbol of unity and peace, having witnessed the city's turbulent past and its reunification. This neoclassical monument is not only an architectural masterpiece but also a reminder of Germany's journey towards democracy. Visitors can walk through the gate and explore the renowned Unter den Linden boulevard, lined with historic buildings and cultural institutions.

No visit to Berlin would be complete without experiencing the poignant history of the Berlin Wall. Once dividing the city, the Wall is now a symbol of triumph over division and a testament to the human spirit. The East Side Gallery, a section of the Wall covered in vibrant murals, is a powerful representation of art and freedom.

Aside from these iconic landmarks, Berlin is also home to world-class museums that delve into various aspects of German history. The Pergamon Museum showcases ancient artifacts, including the famous Ishtar Gate, while the Jewish Museum provides a comprehensive insight into Jewish culture and history.

Furthermore, Berlin is a city of contrasts, where historic buildings blend seamlessly with modern architecture. The Reichstag Building, with its glass dome offering panoramic views of the city, is a testament to this harmonious coexistence.

Beyond its historical significance, Berlin is a vibrant cultural hub. The city boasts a thriving arts scene, with numerous galleries, theaters, and music venues. Visitors can explore the trendy neighborhoods of Kreuzberg and Friedrichshain, known for their vibrant street art and alternative culture.

In addition to its rich history and cultural offerings, Berlin is a city that never sleeps. Its nightlife scene is legendary, with countless bars, clubs, and music festivals catering to every taste.

Whether you're interested in delving into the past, immersing yourself in culture, or simply exploring a city with a unique atmosphere, Berlin is a destination that has it all. From the Brandenburg Gate to the Berlin Wall, this captivating city will leave you with lasting memories and a deeper understanding of Germany's industrial heritage.

Munich: The Residenz and the Marienplatz

Munich, the capital city of Bavaria, is a must-visit destination for any tourist or traveler exploring Germany. In this subchapter, we will uncover two iconic locations in Munich: The Residenz and the Marienplatz.

The Residenz, a former royal palace, is a testament to the grandeur and opulence of Bavarian history. This magnificent complex spans over 130 rooms, each adorned with lavish decorations, intricate artwork, and priceless antiques. As you wander through the Residenz, you will be transported back in time, imagining the lives of Bavarian rulers who once called this place home. Don't miss the Antiquarium, the largest hall in the Residenz, which showcases a collection of ancient Roman sculptures. The Treasury, on the other hand, displays a dazzling array of crown jewels, intricate goldsmith work, and rare artifacts that will leave you awe-struck. The Residenz also houses the Cuvilliés Theatre, a stunning Rococo-style theater that still hosts performances today.

Just a short stroll away from the Residenz is the Marienplatz, Munich's central square and gathering point for locals and visitors alike. This vibrant square is surrounded by remarkable architectural gems, including the New Town Hall, a neo-gothic masterpiece with its famous Glockenspiel. Be sure to arrive at the square at 11 am, 12 pm, or 5 pm to witness the Glockenspiel come to life, as its gurines reenact historical events and folklore tales. The Marienplatz also offers excellent shopping opportunities, with a range of boutique stores, traditional Bavarian markets, and international brands lining the streets.

Aside from its architectural wonders, Munich is also known for its lively beer gardens, where locals and tourists gather to enjoy a cold pint of beer and traditional Bavarian cuisine. The city is also home to the world-famous Oktoberfest, a two-week-long festival celebrating beer, music, and Bavarian culture. During this time, the Theresienwiese, an open space just outside the city center, transforms into a bustling fairground with roller coasters, Ferris wheels, and countless beer tents.

Munich's rich history, stunning landmarks, and vibrant atmosphere make it a top destination for travelers exploring Germany. Whether you're interested in historical sites, cultural festivals, or simply enjoying the beauty of Bavaria, Munich has something to offer everyone. Don't miss the chance to explore the Residenz and experience the lively ambiance of the Marienplatz – two iconic locations that truly capture the essence of this remarkable city.

Cologne: The Cologne Cathedral and the Old Town

In the heart of Germany lies the city of Cologne, a place that seamlessly blends history, culture, and breathtaking architecture. One cannot help but be captivated by the magni cent Cologne Cathedral and the charming Old Town.

The Cologne Cathedral, a UNESCO World Heritage Site, is a true architectural masterpiece. Standing tall at 157 meters, it is a testament to the city's rich history and religious signi cance. As you approach the cathedral, you will be in awe of its Gothic splendor, with intricate details adorning every corner. Step inside, and you will be greeted by the grandeur of the interior, with stained glass windows casting a kaleidoscope of colors. Take the time to climb to the top of the cathedral's south tower, and you will be rewarded with panoramic views of the city and the Rhine River. The Cologne Cathedral is not just a place of worship; it is a symbol of Cologne's resilience and a must- visit for any traveler.

Adjacent to the cathedral lies the Old Town, a vibrant neighborhood that transports you back in time. Wander through its narrow cobblestone streets, lined with colorful half-timbered houses and bustling cafes. The Old Town is a delight for history enthusiasts, with its well-preserved medieval architecture and landmarks. Visit the Historic Town Hall, a masterpiece of Renaissance architecture, or explore the Roman-Germanic Museum, which houses a vast collection of Roman artifacts. Don't forget to stop by the Alter Markt, the central square of the Old Town, where you can soak in the lively atmosphere and indulge in local delicacies at the traditional beer gardens.

Cologne's charm extends beyond its historical sites. The city is known for its vibrant cultural scene, with numerous art galleries, museums, and theaters to explore. Visit the Museum Ludwig, home to an impressive collection of modern and contemporary art, or catch a performance at the Cologne Opera House. For a unique experience, take a stroll along the Rhine River promenade and admire the city's skyline from one of the many riverfront cafes.

Cologne is a city that effortlessly combines its industrial past with its vibrant present. Whether you are a history buff, an art aficionado, or simply seeking a charming city to explore, Cologne's Cologne Cathedral and Old Town will leave an indelible mark on your journey through Germany.

Dresden: The Zwinger Palace and the Frauenkirche

Dresden, the capital city of the state of Saxony in Germany, is a treasure trove of architectural wonders and historical landmarks. Among its many attractions, two sites stand out in particular - the Zwinger Palace and the Frauenkirche. These iconic structures not only showcase the city's rich history but also embody its resilience and determination to rebuild after the devastation of World War II.

The Zwinger Palace, a masterpiece of Baroque architecture, is a sight to behold. Built in the 18th century, it was originally intended as an orangery and pleasure palace for the Saxon royals. Today, it houses a variety of museums, including the Old Masters Picture Gallery, the Porcelain Collection, and the Royal Cabinet of Mathematical and Physical Instruments. As you explore the palace grounds, you'll be captivated by the grandeur of its pavilions, fountains, and gardens. The Zwinger Palace is not just a cultural landmark, but also a symbol of Dresden's artistic and intellectual heritage.

A short walk from the Zwinger Palace will lead you to the Frauenkirche, Dresden's most famous church. Originally built in the 18th century, this stunning Baroque church was destroyed during the bombing of Dresden in 1945. After the reunification of Germany, a massive reconstruction effort was undertaken, and the Frauenkirche was painstakingly restored to its former glory. Today, its magnificent dome and intricate stonework stand as a testament to the city's resilience and the power of hope.

Visiting the Frauenkirche is a deeply moving experience. Step inside and marvel at the breathtaking interior, adorned with ornate altars, delicate stained glass windows, and a majestic organ. Climb to the top of the dome for panoramic views of Dresden's skyline, offering a unique perspective on the city's past and present.

Dresden's Zwinger Palace and Frauenkirche are not just architectural marvels; they are symbols of the city's rich cultural heritage and its ability to rise from the ashes. As a tourist and traveler, exploring these sites will not only give you a glimpse into Germany's history but also inspire you with the resilience and determination of its people. Don't miss the opportunity to visit these exceptional landmarks and discover the beauty and resilience of Dresden.

Hamburg: The St. Michael's Church and the Speicherstadt

As you explore the diverse and captivating destinations in Germany, make sure to add Hamburg to your list of must- visit places. The city is known for its rich industrial heritage, and two standout attractions that showcase this history are the St. Michael's Church and the Speicherstadt warehouse district.

The St. Michael's Church, also known as the "Michel," is a magnificent landmark that dominates the Hamburg skyline. This iconic church dates back to the 17th century and is one of the most important Baroque churches in Northern Germany. Its towering copper roof and impressive clock tower make it a sight to behold.

Step inside the church and marvel at its stunning interior, adorned with intricate woodwork, marble columns, and beautiful stained glass windows. Take the opportunity to climb up the tower for a panoramic view of the city and the bustling Port of Hamburg. On clear days, you can even catch a glimpse of the neighboring city of Lübeck.

Just a short walk from St. Michael's Church, you'll find the Speicherstadt, a historic warehouse district that has been designated as a UNESCO World Heritage Site. This extraordinary complex of red-brick buildings, canals, and bridges was once the heart of Hamburg's thriving trading industry.

Explore the narrow streets and discover the charming coffee houses, shops, and museums that now occupy these former warehouses. The Speicherstadt is particularly famous for its carpet stores, where you can find exquisite hand-woven rugs from all over the world.

For an even more immersive experience, take a boat tour through the canals of the Speicherstadt. Admire the unique architecture reflected in the water and learn about the district's fascinating history from knowledgeable guides. As you glide along, you'll pass by massive ships unloading their cargo, providing a glimpse into Hamburg's continuing role as a major seaport.

Hamburg's St. Michael's Church and the Speicherstadt warehouse district are not only important symbols of the city's industrial past but also offer visitors a chance to experience the unique charm and history of this vibrant metropolis. Make sure to include these remarkable sites in your itinerary and discover the captivating stories they have to tell.

Frankfurt: The Römer and the Goethe House

One of the top 15 places to visit in Germany is the vibrant city of Frankfurt. While known for its modern skyline and nancial district, Frankfurt also offers a rich historical experience. Two must-visit attractions that showcase the city's history are the Römer and the Goethe House.

The Römer is a historic building complex located in Frankfurt's Old Town. Dating back to the 15th century, it has served as Frankfurt's city hall for over 600 years. Its iconic three-gabled facade and the courtyard with its beautiful fountain make it a true architectural gem. Visitors can explore the various rooms and chambers, each decorated with intricate woodwork and historical artifacts. The Römer is also home to the Imperial Hall, where emperors were once elected and crowned.

Not far from the Römer is the Goethe House, the birthplace of Germany's most famous writer, Johann Wolfgang von Goethe. This half-timbered house has been meticulously restored to its original 18th-century appearance, allowing visitors to step back in time and immerse themselves in the world of Goethe. Inside, you can explore the rooms where Goethe grew up, including his bedroom, study, and even his father's pharmacy. The museum also houses a vast collection of Goethe's personal belongings, manuscripts, and artworks.

Both the Römer and the Goethe House provide a glimpse into different eras of Frankfurt's history. The Römer represents the city's medieval past and its importance as a political and economic center, while the Goethe House showcases the cultural and literary heritage of Germany.

Visiting these historical landmarks allows tourists and travelers to gain a deeper understanding of Frankfurt's past and its significant contributions to German history. Whether you are interested in architecture, politics, or literature, these sites offer a fascinating journey through time.

In conclusion, the Rome and the Goethe House are essential stops on any trip to Frankfurt. They offer a unique blend of history, culture, and architecture that will captivate tourists and travelers alike. By exploring these sites, visitors can appreciate the rich heritage of Germany and the role Frankfurt played in shaping the country's past.

Leipzig: The St. Thomas Church and the Battle of the Nations Monument

Leipzig, a vibrant city in eastern Germany, offers a unique blend of history, culture, and natural beauty. As a tourist and traveler exploring Germany's top destinations, you must not miss the St. Thomas Church and the Battle of the Nation's Monument in Leipzig. These iconic landmarks represent Leipzig's rich history and its significance in shaping Germany's past.

The St. Thomas Church, with its striking Gothic architecture, is famous for its association with Johann Sebastian Bach, one of the greatest composers of all time. This historic church served as Bach's workplace for almost three decades. Today, it is a revered concert venue, hosting performances of Bach's masterpieces and other classical music. As you step inside, you can feel the grandeur of the church's interior and admire the magnificent organ that Bach himself played.

Adjacent to the St. Thomas Church stands the Battle of the Nations Monument, a colossal structure that commemorates the decisive Battle of Leipzig in 1813. This battle was a turning point in the Napoleonic Wars, leading to the defeat of Napoleon Bonaparte. The monument, standing at an impressive height of 91 meters, offers panoramic views of Leipzig. You can climb to the top and marvel at the surrounding landscape while reflecting on the historical significance of this site.

Leipzig itself is a city steeped in history. Known as the "City of Heroes," it played a vital role in the peaceful revolution of 1989 that led to the fall of the Berlin Wall and the reunification of Germany. Walking through the city, you will encounter beautiful architecture, charming squares, and a vibrant arts scene. The Leipzig Gewandhaus Orchestra, one of the world's finest, calls this city home, and its performances are not to be missed.

Leipzig's location in the state of Saxony also offers easy access to other historical cities such as Dresden and Meissen, known for their world-renowned porcelain. A visit to these cities would allow you to delve deeper into Germany's rich cultural heritage.

As a tourist and traveler, exploring Leipzig and its iconic landmarks, including the St. Thomas Church and the Battle of the Nations Monument, will provide you with a deeper understanding of Germany's history and its significance in shaping the world we live in today. So, make sure to add Leipzig to your list of must-visit places in Germany, and prepare to be captivated by its historical charm and cultural richness.

Chapter 3: Fairy Tale Castles: Discover the Enchanting Neuschwanstein Castle and Other Fairytale-like Castles Scattered across Germany

Neuschwanstein Castle: Ludwig II's Fairytale Dream

Perched on a hilltop in the picturesque Bavarian region of Germany, Neuschwanstein Castle is a true embodiment of a fairy tale dream. Built in the late 19th century by King Ludwig II of Bavaria, this enchanting castle continues to captivate the hearts of visitors from around the world.

As you approach Neuschwanstein Castle, you will be greeted by its majestic towers, turrets, and spires, rising against the backdrop of the breathtaking Bavarian Alps. The castle's design was heavily influenced by the romantic ideals of the Middle Ages, with its grandeur and intricate detailing resembling something straight out of a storybook.

Step inside the castle, and you will be transported to a world of opulence and fantasy. The interior of Neuschwanstein Castle is just as impressive as its exterior, with lavishly decorated rooms showcasing Ludwig II's obsession with Wagnerian opera and medieval legends. From the Throne Room, adorned with gold leaf and vibrant frescoes, to the ethereal beauty of the Singers' Hall, every inch of the castle exudes a sense of magic and wonder.

Neuschwanstein Castle's allure goes beyond its architectural splendor. It is also a place of inspiration, having served as the model for Disney's Sleeping Beauty Castle. As you explore the castle and its surrounding grounds, you can't help but feel like you've stepped into a fairytale yourself.

But Neuschwanstein Castle is not the only fairytale-like castle to discover in Germany. Travelers can also immerse themselves in the romance and history of other castles, such as Heidelberg Castle, perched above the Neckar River, or Hohenzollern Castle, set amidst the rolling hills of the Swabian Alps.

For those seeking to experience the magic of Germany, visiting Neuschwanstein Castle is an absolute must. It allows you to be transported back in time to a world of knights, princesses, and a fairytale romance. Whether you are a history enthusiast, a lover of architecture, or simply someone looking to be swept away by the charm of a bygone era, Neuschwanstein Castle promises an unforgettable experience that will leave you feeling like you've just stepped out of a storybook.

Heidelberg Castle: A Symbol of Romanticism

One of the most iconic and enchanting castles in Germany, Heidelberg Castle stands as a symbol of romanticism and captivates the hearts of tourists and travelers alike. Located in the picturesque city of Heidelberg, this fairytale-like castle transports visitors back in time to a world of medieval charm and breathtaking beauty.

Perched high above the Neckar River, Heidelberg Castle offers panoramic views of the surrounding landscapes, creating a truly magical experience. Its architectural grandeur and impressive ruins make it a must-visit destination for those seeking to immerse themselves in Germany's rich history and romantic atmosphere.

Originally built in the 13th century, Heidelberg Castle was once home to the powerful Prince Electors of the Palatinate. Throughout the centuries, it underwent expansions and renovations, resulting in a unique blend of Gothic, Renaissance, and Baroque styles. Today, visitors can explore the castle's various sections, including the Great Hall, the German Pharmacy Museum, and the impressive gardens.

One of the highlights of a visit to Heidelberg Castle is the renowned Heidelberg Tun, the world's largest wine barrel. With a capacity of over 200,000 liters, this enormous barrel is a testament to Germany's rich wine culture and offers a fascinating glimpse into the region's viticulture history.

Aside from its architectural marvels, Heidelberg Castle is also steeped in legends and stories of romance. The tale of the "Heidelberg Tun" and the love story of Frederick V, the Winter King, and his wife Elizabeth Stuart, the Queen of Hearts, adds a touch of romanticism to the castle's allure.

Surrounded by the idyllic charm of Heidelberg's cobblestone streets and half-timbered houses, a visit to Heidelberg Castle is a journey into a world of fairy tales and romance. Whether strolling through the castle's gardens, exploring its historic interiors, or simply admiring the breathtaking views, this iconic landmark is a must-see for any traveler seeking to experience the magic of Germany.

In conclusion, Heidelberg Castle is a true gem of Germany's romantic landscape. Its rich history, architectural splendor, and stunning views make it a top destination for tourists and travelers exploring the country's enchanting castles. Whether you are a history enthusiast, a lover of fairy tales, or simply seeking a romantic getaway, a visit to Heidelberg Castle is sure to leave you spellbound.

Hohenzollern Castle: A Fortress in the Swabian Alps

Perched atop a hill in the Swabian Alps, Hohenzollern Castle stands as a majestic fortress that transports visitors back in time. This fairy tale-like castle is one of Germany's most iconic landmarks and a must-visit destination for tourists and travelers alike.

Built in the 11th century, Hohenzollern Castle has a rich history that reflects the power and influence of the Hohenzollern dynasty. Over the centuries, the castle was destroyed and rebuilt multiple times, resulting in its current impressive neo-Gothic architectural style. As you approach the castle, you'll be captivated by its grandeur, with its towers, turrets, and battlements reaching towards the sky.

Stepping inside, you'll be transported even further into the past as you explore the castle's interior. Admire the opulent rooms adorned with exquisite tapestries, antique furniture, and intricate woodwork. Marvel at the stunning views of the surrounding countryside from the castle's terraces, which offer breathtaking panoramas of the Swabian Alps.

Hohenzollern Castle is not only a visual delight but also a treasure trove of historical artifacts. The castle houses a vast collection of weapons, armor, and artwork, providing a glimpse into the lives of the Hohenzollern family throughout the centuries. Visitors can also learn about the castle's strategic importance during times of war and its role in shaping the region's history.

Aside from its historical significance, Hohenzollern Castle offers a truly magical experience. Immerse yourself in the castle's enchanting atmosphere as you stroll through its picturesque gardens, filled with colorful flowers and meticulously manicured hedges. You can even witness a medieval reenactment or a traditional festival, adding to the castle's allure.

For those seeking a unique and unforgettable experience in Germany, Hohenzollern Castle is a must-visit destination. Its combination of rich history, stunning architecture, and breathtaking surroundings make it one of the top 15 places to visit in the country. Whether you're a history enthusiast, a lover of fairy tale castles, or simply in search of a picturesque escape, Hohenzollern Castle will leave you awe-inspired and longing to return.

Linderhof Palace: Extravagance and Elegance

In the heart of the Bavarian Alps lies a place of unparalleled extravagance and elegance – Linderhof Palace. This magnificent palace, located near the town of Ettal, is a must-visit destination for any tourist or traveler seeking to immerse themselves in the opulent world of German royalty.

Built by King Ludwig II of Bavaria in the 19th century, Linderhof Palace is a true testament to the king's love for beauty, art, and grandeur. As you approach the palace, you will be greeted by its stunning Baroque architecture, adorned with intricate details and elaborate decorations. The palace's perfectly manicured gardens, inspired by the iconic French gardens of Versailles, are a sight to behold, with fountains, statues, and meticulously arranged flowerbeds creating a picture-perfect landscape.

Step inside the palace, and you will be transported to a world of luxury and indulgence. The opulent interiors, featuring lavish furnishings, ornate ceilings, and exquisite artwork, are a reflection of the king's refined taste and passion for the arts. Explore the various rooms, including the Hall of Mirrors, the King's Bedroom, and the Oriental Cabinet, each offering a glimpse into the king's extravagant lifestyle.

One of the highlights of a visit to Linderhof Palace is the tour of the King's Study, a private sanctuary where Ludwig II would retreat to immerse himself in literature and music. This intimate space, adorned with gold leaf and adorned with intricate woodwork, provides a fascinating insight into the king's personal interests and passions.

After exploring the palace, take a stroll through the palace grounds and discover the various outbuildings and structures that complement the grandeur of Linderhof. Visit the stunning Venus Grotto, an arti cial cave adorned with stalactites and a lake, where the king would enjoy private concerts and performances. The Moroccan House, a charming pavilion inspired by the oriental architecture, is another hidden gem worth exploring.

Linderhof Palace is not only a testament to the extravagance of German royalty but also a window into the history and culture of the Bavarian region. As you walk through the palace and its grounds, you will be transported to a bygone era of grandeur and elegance, leaving you with a newfound appreciation for the rich heritage of Germany.

Visiting Linderhof Palace is an essential part of any traveler's journey through Germany. Its combination of architectural beauty, stunning gardens, and historical significance makes it one of the top 15 places to visit in the country. So, add Linderhof Palace to your itinerary and prepare to be captivated by its extravagance and elegance.

Wartburg Castle: Medieval History and Martin Luther's Hideout

Located in the scenic hills of Thuringia, Wartburg Castle is a captivating destination that offers a glimpse into Germany's medieval history and the tumultuous life of Martin Luther. As one of the top 15 places to visit in Germany, this historic castle holds a special place in the hearts of tourists and travelers seeking an authentic cultural experience.

Stepping into Wartburg Castle is like stepping back in time. The castle boasts a rich history that dates back to the 11th century, making it one of Germany's oldest surviving castles. Its impressive architecture and well-preserved interior transport visitors to a bygone era, where knights roamed the halls and troubadours serenaded noble ladies.

But Wartburg Castle's significance goes beyond its medieval charm. It served as a refuge for Martin Luther during his exile in the 16th century. It was within these walls that Luther translated the New Testament into German, a monumental achievement that forever
changed the course of Christianity. Visitors can explore the room where Luther worked, gaining insight into the pivotal role he played in the Protestant Reformation.

Aside from its historical allure, Wartburg Castle also offers breathtaking views of the surrounding countryside. Perched atop a hill, it overlooks the picturesque town of Eisenach and the lush Thuringian Forest. The castle's idyllic setting makes it a perfect spot for romantic walks and photo opportunities.

To enhance the visitor experience, Wartburg Castle hosts various events and exhibitions throughout the year. From medieval festivals showcasing jousting tournaments and period costumes to art exhibitions that delve into the castle's past, there is always something new and exciting happening at Wartburg Castle.

For those interested in delving deeper into Germany's industrial heritage, Wartburg Castle is a must-visit destination. Its medieval history and association with Martin Luther makes it a standout attraction among the country's top historical sites. So, whether you're a history buff, a lover of fairy tale castles, or simply a curious traveler, be sure to add Wartburg Castle to your itinerary and immerse yourself in the rich tapestry of Germany's cultural heritage.

Chapter 4: Romantic Villages: Experience the Idyllic Charm of German Villages like Rothenburg ob der Tauber and Cochem

Rothenburg ob der Tauber: Half-timbered Houses and the Romantic Road

One of the top 15 places to visit in Germany as a tourist is the enchanting village of Rothenburg ob der Tauber. Located along the famous Romantic Road, this picturesque village is known for its half-timbered houses, cobblestone streets, and idyllic charm.

As you wander through the streets of Rothenburg ob der Tauber, you'll feel like you've stepped back in time. The village is filled with well-preserved medieval architecture, with many buildings dating back to the 16th century. The half-timbered houses, with their intricate woodwork and colorful facades, create a fairytale-like atmosphere that is truly captivating.

One of the highlights of Rothenburg ob der Tauber is the Plönlein, a picturesque square that is often considered one of the most beautiful spots in Germany. Here, you can admire the iconic Kobolzeller Tower and the Siebers Tower, which frame the square and provide a stunning backdrop for photos.

Another must-visit attraction in Rothenburg ob der Tauber is the Town Hall, a magnificent building that showcases the town's rich history. Inside, you can explore the Imperial Hall, adorned with beautiful frescoes, and learn about the town's role in medieval trade and commerce.

Rothenburg ob der Tauber is also famous for its Christmas market, which attracts visitors from all over the world. The market takes place in the town's main square and offers a magical atmosphere with its festive decorations, traditional crafts, and delicious treats.

If you're a fan of history, Rothenburg ob der Tauber has a wealth of museums to explore. The Medieval Crime Museum delves into the dark side of medieval justice, while the Doll and Toy Museum showcases a collection of antique dolls and toys.

To fully experience the beauty of Rothenburg ob der Tauber, take a stroll along the town walls. From here, you can enjoy panoramic views of the village and the surrounding countryside, making for a truly memorable experience.

Rothenburg ob der Tauber is a must-visit destination for anyone seeking to explore Germany's romantic villages and immerse themselves in the country's rich history. With its half-timbered houses, cobblestone streets, and enchanting atmosphere, this village is sure to capture your heart and leave you with lasting memories.

Cochem: A Picturesque Town along the Mosel River

Nestled along the winding Mosel River, the picturesque town of Cochem is a hidden gem in Germany's industrial heritage. This charming town is a must-visit destination for tourists and travelers seeking a blend of history, natural beauty, and a touch of fairy tale charm.

Cochem is a part of the top 15 places to visit in Germany as a tourist for its unique blend of historical signi cance and idyllic landscapes. The town is known for its half-timbered houses, cobblestone streets, and panoramic views of the Mosel River. As you stroll through the town, you'll feel like you've stepped into a storybook, with every corner offering a picture-perfect scene.

The highlight of Cochem is undoubtedly the majestic Cochem Castle, perched high on a hill overlooking the town. This medieval fortress dates back to the 11th century and offers breathtaking views of the surrounding vineyards and the Mosel Valley. Take a guided tour of the castle and immerse yourself in its rich history, or simply enjoy the stunning views from its terraces.

Speaking of vineyards, Cochem is also renowned for its wine production. Located in the heart of the Mosel wine region, the town is surrounded by lush vineyards that produce some of Germany's nest wines. Take a leisurely stroll through the vineyards, visit local wineries for tastings, and experience the region's wine culture firsthand.

In addition to its natural beauty and wine culture, Cochem also offers a glimpse into Germany's industrial heritage. While the town itself may not have a significant industrial past, it serves as a gateway to the nearby Zollverein Coal Mine Industrial Complex in Essen. This UNESCO World Heritage Site offers a fascinating insight into Germany's coal mining history and is a must-visit for history enthusiasts.

Whether you're exploring the historical cities, discovering fairy tale castles, or indulging in the country's renowned wine culture, a visit to Cochem should be high on your list. Its picturesque landscapes, charming architecture, and rich history make it a truly special destination. So, pack your bags, embark on a journey, and let the enchanting town of Cochem captivate your heart.

Bamberg: Medieval Architecture and the Bamberg Cathedral

Located in the heart of Bavaria, Bamberg is a hidden gem that should not be missed on any traveler's itinerary. This picturesque city is known for its well-preserved medieval architecture and is often referred to as a living museum. One of its most iconic landmarks is the Bamberg Cathedral, a masterpiece of medieval architecture that stands proudly in the city center.

The Bamberg Cathedral, also known as the Bamberger Dom, is a UNESCO World Heritage Site and a testament to the city's rich history. Built in the 13th century, the cathedral's stunning exterior features a mix of Romanesque and Gothic styles, making it a true architectural marvel. Its towering spires and intricate stone carvings will leave visitors in awe.

Inside the cathedral, visitors will find a treasure trove of art and history. The highlight is the Bamberg Horseman, a statue believed to be the oldest equestrian statue in Europe. The statue is shrouded in mystery, with its origins and meaning still debated by historians. Other notable features include the tomb of Emperor Henry II and his wife, Cunigunde, as well as beautiful stained glass windows that depict biblical scenes.

Beyond the cathedral, Bamberg is a city that begs to be explored. Its charming old town, known as the Altstadt, is a maze of cobblestone streets and half-timbered houses. Visitors can wander through the narrow alleys and discover quaint shops, traditional breweries, and cozy cafes. The city's seven hills offer breathtaking views of the surrounding countryside, and the Regnitz River adds a touch of romance to the scenery.

For those interested in history, Bamberg offers a wealth of museums and historical sites. The Altes Rathaus, or Old Town Hall, is a unique building that straddles the river and is a symbol of the city. The Franconian Brewery Museum provides insight into Bamberg's brewing heritage, while the Historical Museum showcases the city's past through a rich collection of artifacts.

Bamberg is truly a city that transports visitors back in time. With its medieval architecture, rich history, and unique charm, it is a must-visit destination for any traveler exploring Germany. Whether you are a history buff, an architecture enthusiast, or simply looking for a picturesque getaway, Bamberg will not disappoint. So, make sure to add it to your list of top places to visit in Germany and experience the magic of this medieval gem for yourself.

Quedlinburg: Timber-framed Houses and Historic Charm

Nestled in the picturesque Harz Mountains, the town of Quedlinburg is a hidden gem that showcases the rich history and architectural beauty of Germany. With its timber-framed houses and cobblestone streets, Quedlinburg is a fairy tale come to life, offering visitors a glimpse into the country's medieval past.

As you wander through the narrow, winding streets of Quedlinburg, it's easy to imagine yourself stepping back in time. The town's well-preserved timber-framed houses, some dating back over 600 years, are a testament to its historical significance. Each house tells a story, with their intricate carvings, colorful facades, and charming courtyards. The entire town is a UNESCO World Heritage site, recognized for its exceptional architectural heritage.

One of the highlights of a visit to Quedlinburg is the Quedlinburg Castle, perched atop a hill overlooking the town. This magnificent medieval castle offers breathtaking views of the surrounding countryside and houses a museum that delves into the town's history. From here, you can also explore the nearby St. Servatius' Church, a Romanesque masterpiece that houses priceless treasures, including one of the oldest surviving medieval crypts in Germany.

Quedlinburg is also famous for its annual Christmas market, which transforms the town into a winter wonderland during the holiday season. Stroll through the market, savoring the aromas of gingerbread and mulled wine, while admiring the festive decorations and listening to carolers. It's a magical experience that shouldn't be missed.

For those interested in delving deeper into Quedlinburg's history, a visit to the Fachwerkmuseum is a must. This museum showcases the craftsmanship and techniques used in constructing timber-framed houses, providing a fascinating insight into the town's architectural heritage.

Quedlinburg is a place where history comes alive, where every corner reveals a story waiting to be discovered. Whether you're a history enthusiast, an architecture lover, or simply seeking a charming and romantic getaway, Quedlinburg is a destination that will captivate your heart and leave you with memories to cherish for a lifetime.

Chapter 5: Wine Regions: Indulge in Germany's Renowned Wine Culture by Visiting Regions like the Mosel Valley or the Rheingau

Mosel Valley: Riesling Vineyards and Breathtaking Scenery

The Mosel Valley is a gem nestled in the heart of Germany, renowned for its exquisite Riesling vineyards and breathtaking scenery. This subchapter explores the enchanting beauty of this region, perfect for those seeking a unique and unforgettable experience.

As you journey through the Mosel Valley, you will be captivated by the lush green vineyards that stretch as far as the eye can see. This region is famed for producing some of the finest Riesling wines in the world, thanks to its cool climate and slate-rich soils. Wine enthusiasts will delight in visiting renowned wineries, learning about the winemaking process, and indulging in wine tastings that showcase the distinct flavors and aromas of the Mosel Valley.

But it's not just the wine that makes this region special. The Mosel River meanders through the valley, offering stunning views at every turn. Take a leisurely cruise along the river, and you'll be treated to postcard-perfect landscapes of vine-covered hillsides, charming villages, and medieval castles perched on hilltops. The sight of the sun setting over the river, casting a golden glow on the surrounding vineyards, is truly a sight to behold.

For the adventurous souls, the Mosel Valley offers a plethora of outdoor activities. Embark on a hike along the Moselsteig trail, which winds its way through the valley, offering panoramic views and opportunities to explore hidden gems along the way. Cyclists can pedal along the Moselle Cycle Path, which follows the river and takes you through picturesque towns and vineyards.

The Mosel Valley is also known for its vibrant wine festivals, where locals and visitors come together to celebrate the region's rich winemaking heritage. From the Bernkastel-Kues Wine Festival to the Cochem Wine Week, these events offer a chance to immerse yourself in the lively atmosphere, taste a variety of wines, and revel in traditional music and dancing.

Whether you're a wine lover, an outdoor enthusiast, or simply seeking a serene escape amidst breathtaking landscapes, the Mosel Valley is an absolute must-visit. It combines the best of Germany's wine culture with stunning natural beauty, making it a top destination for tourists and travelers alike. So, raise a glass of Riesling and toast to the splendors of the Mosel Valley – a true paradise for wine connoisseurs and nature enthusiasts.

Rheingau: Wine Festivals and Historic Castles

The Rheingau region in Germany is a hidden gem that combines the pleasures of wine with the allure of history. Situated along the banks of the Rhine River, this stunning region is known for its vineyards, wine festivals, and picturesque castles. Whether you are a wine connoisseur or a history buff, the Rheingau has something to offer for everyone.

The Rheingau is renowned for its wine culture, and visiting this region is a must for any wine lover. With its mild climate and fertile soil, the Rheingau produces some of Germany's nest wines. Take a tour of the vineyards and learn about the winemaking process from knowledgeable experts. Stop by one of the many wine festivals held throughout the year, where you can taste a variety of wines and immerse yourself in the vibrant atmosphere.

But it's not just about the wine in the Rheingau – the region is also home to a number of historic castles that are sure to transport you back in time. Explore the sprawling grounds of Schloss Johannisberg, a castle that dates back to the 12th century. Marvel at the medieval architecture of Burg Eltville, which offers panoramic views of the surrounding vineyards. And don't miss a visit to Schloss Vollrads, one of the oldest wine estates in the world, where you can wander through its enchanting gardens and sample their award-winning wines.

In addition to wine and castles, the Rheingau boasts breathtaking landscapes that are perfect for outdoor enthusiasts. Take a leisurely stroll along the Rhine River and soak in the stunning views of the vineyards and rolling hills. Or, for a more adventurous experience, embark on a scenic hike through the Rheingau-Taunus Nature Park, where you can discover hidden gems like the Niederwald Monument and the Rüdesheim Cable Car.

For the ultimate Rheingau experience, plan your visit during one of the region's wine festivals. The Rheingau Wine Festival, held annually in Wiesbaden, is a celebration of the region's wine culture and features live music, culinary delights, and of course, plenty of wine tasting. The Rüdesheim Wine Festival is another popular event, where locals and tourists come together to celebrate the harvest season with traditional music, dance, and wine tastings.

Whether you are a wine enthusiast, a history lover, or simply someone looking for a unique travel experience, the Rheingau has it all. From its world-class wines to its historic castles, this region offers a perfect blend of culture, history, and natural beauty. So raise a glass and toast to the wonders of the Rheingau – a destination that truly captures the essence of Germany's industrial heritage.

Baden: Pinot Noir and Thermal Baths

In the southwestern region of Germany lies the picturesque town of Baden, a hidden gem that combines the pleasures of fine wine with the relaxation of thermal baths. For those seeking a unique and indulgent experience, Baden offers the perfect blend of luxury and tranquility.

Known as one of the top wine regions in Germany, Baden is famous for its exquisite Pinot Noir. The region's mild climate and fertile soil create the ideal conditions for cultivating this delicate and flavorful wine. Wine enthusiasts will delight in exploring the vineyards, tasting the rich variety of Pinot Noir, and learning about the centuries-old winemaking traditions.

After indulging in the flavors of Baden's renowned wine culture, visitors can unwind and rejuvenate in the town's thermal baths. Baden is home to some of the most exquisite spa retreats in Germany, where thermal waters enriched with minerals and healing properties provide a soothing oasis for the body and mind. Immerse yourself in the warm waters, release tension with a relaxing massage, or simply soak up the tranquil atmosphere of these rejuvenating havens.

Beyond the vineyards and thermal baths, Baden also offers a charming town center filled with historic buildings, quaint streets, and vibrant markets. Stroll through the cobblestone streets, admire the half-timbered houses, and indulge in local delicacies at the bustling marketplaces. Don't miss the opportunity to visit the grand Kurhaus, a magnificent 19th-century spa complex that boasts stunning architecture and hosts various cultural events throughout the year.

For nature enthusiasts, Baden is surrounded by breathtaking landscapes that invite exploration. The nearby Black Forest offers endless opportunities for hiking, biking, and immersing oneself in the beauty of nature. Explore dense forests, crystal-clear lakes, and picturesque trails that lead to stunning viewpoints. Take a leisurely boat ride along the Rhine River or venture further to the enchanting Lake Constance, where the beauty of nature merges with the charm of historic towns.

Whether you're a wine lover, a spa enthusiast, or simply seeking a serene escape, Baden promises an unforgettable experience. Discover the rich flavors of Pinot Noir, surrender to the healing powers of thermal baths, and immerse yourself in the enchanting landscapes of this hidden paradise. Baden is a true haven for those seeking a perfect blend of indulgence, relaxation, and natural beauty.

Franconia: Silvaner Wine and Romantic Vineyard Landscapes

In the heart of Germany, nestled between picturesque vineyards and rolling hills, lies Franconia, a region renowned for its exquisite Silvaner wine and breathtaking vineyard landscapes. For tourists and travelers seeking a unique and romantic experience, Franconia is a must-visit destination that will captivate both your taste buds and your soul.

The star of Franconia's wine production is the Silvaner grape, which thrives in the region's fertile soil and cool climate. Known for its crispness, elegance, and subtle avors, the Silvaner wine produced here has gained international acclaim. Wine enthusiasts can explore the countless vineyards and wineries that dot the landscape, where they can learn about the winemaking process, sample different varieties of Silvaner, and even participate in wine tasting events and festivals.

But it's not just the wine that makes Franconia special. The region's vineyard landscapes are nothing short of enchanting. As you wander through the vineyards, you'll be greeted by row upon row of meticulously cultivated vines, stretching as far as the eye can see. The terraced vineyards, with their neatly arranged stone walls, create a stunning visual spectacle and offer panoramic views of the surrounding countryside. Whether you're a wine connoisseur or simply a lover of natural beauty, the vineyard landscapes of Franconia are sure to leave you in awe.

Aside from wine and vineyards, Franconia also offers a wealth of cultural and historical attractions. Explore the charming towns and villages that dot the region, each with its own unique charm and character. Visit historical sites like the Würzburg Residence, a UNESCO World Heritage Site and one of Germany's nest Baroque palaces. Take a stroll through the medieval streets of Rothenburg ob der Tauber, with its well-preserved half-timbered houses and cobblestone lanes. Or immerse yourself in the lively atmosphere of Nuremberg's famous Christmas markets, where you can shop for traditional handicrafts and indulge in delicious local treats.

Whether you're a wine lover, a history buff, or simply someone in search of natural beauty, Franconia has something to offer. Its Silvaner wine and romantic vineyard landscapes make it a unique and unforgettable destination. So pack your bags, grab a glass of wine, and get ready to discover the beauty of Franconia.

Chapter 6: Alpine Retreats: Unwind in the Breathtaking Beauty of the Bavarian Alps

Garmisch-Partenkirchen: Outdoor Adventures and Zugspitze Peak

Located in the heart of the Bavarian Alps, Garmisch-Partenkirchen is a paradise for outdoor enthusiasts and nature lovers. This picturesque town offers an array of exciting activities and breathtaking landscapes that will captivate the hearts of tourists and travelers alike.

A highlight of Garmisch-Partenkirchen is the majestic Zugspitze Peak, which stands at an impressive 2,962 meters above sea level. As the highest mountain in Germany, Zugspitze offers visitors a thrilling experience and panoramic views that are second to none. Whether you are an avid hiker or prefer a more leisurely cable car ride, reaching the summit is an adventure you won't want to miss.

For those seeking an adrenaline rush, Garmisch-Partenkirchen is a haven for winter sports enthusiasts. With its world-class ski resorts and well-maintained slopes, the town attracts skiers and snowboarders from around the globe. From beginners to experts, there are slopes suitable for every level, ensuring an unforgettable winter getaway.

During the summer months, Garmisch-Partenkirchen transforms into a haven for hikers and climbers. The region offers a network of trails that wind through lush meadows, dense forests, and stunning alpine landscapes. Whether you are a seasoned mountaineer or simply enjoy a leisurely stroll, there are hiking routes for all abilities. Don't miss the opportunity to explore the Partnach Gorge, a natural wonder that will leave you in awe of its beauty.

Beyond its outdoor adventures, Garmisch-Partenkirchen is also known for its charming Bavarian architecture and warm hospitality. The town's traditional half-timbered houses, cobblestone streets, and vibrant markets create a fairy tale-like atmosphere that transports visitors back in time. Immerse yourself in the local culture by sampling Bavarian delicacies, exploring the local shops, or attending one of the many cultural festivals that take place throughout the year.

Garmisch-Partenkirchen perfectly embodies the spirit of the Bavarian Alps, offering a range of activities and experiences that cater to all interests. Whether you are an outdoor enthusiast, a history buff, or simply seeking a peaceful retreat, this enchanting town has something to offer everyone. So, pack your bags, put on your hiking boots, and get ready to embark on an unforgettable adventure in Garmisch-Partenkirchen, where nature's beauty and exhilarating activities await.

Berchtesgaden: Natural Beauty and Historical Significance

Nestled in the heart of the Bavarian Alps, Berchtesgaden is a destination that showcases the natural beauty and historical significance of Germany. This picturesque town offers a perfect blend of stunning landscapes, outdoor activities, and a rich historical past, making it a must-visit place for tourists and travelers seeking a unique experience.

The natural beauty of Berchtesgaden is unparalleled. Surrounded by majestic mountains, lush green valleys, and crystal-clear lakes, it is a paradise for nature lovers. The Berchtesgaden National Park, with its diverse flora and fauna, offers numerous hiking trails, allowing visitors to explore the breathtaking landscapes and enjoy panoramic views of the surrounding mountains.

One of the highlights of Berchtesgaden is the famous Königssee, a pristine lake nestled amidst towering mountains. Known for its emerald-green waters, the Königssee offers boat tours that take visitors to the iconic St. Bartholomew's Church, a picturesque pilgrimage site dating back to the 12th century.

In addition to its natural beauty, Berchtesgaden also holds great historical significance. The town was once a favorite retreat for Adolf Hitler, and remnants of his presence can still be seen today. The Eagle's Nest, perched high on a mountain peak, was Hitler's former mountain retreat and now serves as a historical site offering panoramic views of the surrounding Alps.

For history enthusiasts, a visit to the Documentation Center Obersalzberg is a must. This museum provides a comprehensive insight into the rise and fall of the Nazi regime, showcasing original artifacts and documents from that era.

Berchtesgaden also offers opportunities for outdoor activities such as skiing, snowboarding, and hiking. The Jennerbahn cable car takes visitors to the top of Mount Jenner, where they can enjoy breathtaking views and explore the Alpine landscapes.

With its natural beauty, historical significance, and outdoor activities, Berchtesgaden truly deserves a spot on the list of top places to visit in Germany. Whether it's immersing in the tranquility of the mountains, exploring the historical sites, or indulging in outdoor adventures, Berchtesgaden offers a unique and unforgettable experience for all types of travelers.

Oberammergau: Passion Plays and Traditional Woodcarving

One of the hidden gems of Germany that combines a unique cultural experience with exquisite craftsmanship is the charming village of Oberammergau. Nestled in the heart of the Bavarian Alps, this picturesque town is renowned for its Passion Plays and traditional woodcarving.

Every ten years, the residents of Oberammergau come together to perform the world-famous Passion Play. This religious spectacle, which dates back to 1634, depicts the life, death, and resurrection of Jesus Christ. The entire village participates in this grand production, with over 2,000 actors, musicians, and technicians taking part. The Passion Play is a testament to the unwavering commitment and talent of the local community, and it attracts visitors from all over the world. The next performance is scheduled for 2022, so make sure to plan your visit accordingly.

In addition to the Passion Play, Oberammergau is also renowned for its traditional woodcarving. The town boasts a rich history of craftsmanship that dates back to the 17th century. Wander through the streetsand you'll find numerous shops and workshops where talented artisans create intricate woodcarvings. From religious figures to intricate nativity scenes, the craftsmanship on display is truly awe-inspiring. Visitors have the opportunity to witness the artists at work and even purchase unique wooden souvenirs to take home.

Beyond the Passion Plays and woodcarving, Oberammergau offers a myriad of other attractions. The surrounding alpine landscape provides ample opportunities for outdoor activities such as hiking, skiing, and mountain biking. The town is also home to a number of charming guesthouses and restaurants, where visitors can indulge in traditional Bavarian cuisine.

For those interested in history and culture, Oberammergau is a must-visit destination. Immerse yourself in the centuries-old tradition of the Passion Play and witness the extraordinary craftsmanship of the woodcarvers. This small village offers a truly unique and unforgettable experience that is sure to leave a lasting impression. So, make sure to include Oberammergau in your itinerary when exploring the beauty of Germany.

Chapter 7: Cultural Festivals: Immerse Yourself in German Traditions and Festivities

Oktoberfest in Munich is the world's largest beer festival and a must-visit event for any beer enthusiast or lover of German culture. Every year, millions of people from around the globe flock to this vibrant city to indulge in the festivities, taste traditional Bavarian cuisine, and immerse themselves in the lively atmosphere.

The heart of Oktoberfest is the Theresienwiese, a massive fairground that transforms into a beer lover's paradise during the festival. Here, you'll find row upon row of colorful beer tents, each offering a unique selection of Bavarian brews. From traditional pilsners to rich and malty Blocks, there's a beer to suit every taste. Grab a stein, raise it high, and join in the cheerful "prost" (cheers) with fellow festival-goers.

No visit to Oktoberfest would be complete without indulging in some mouthwatering Bavarian cuisine. Savor the aroma of sizzling bratwursts, pretzels as big as your head, and crispy schnitzels. Take a seat at one of the long communal tables and dig in, enjoying the camaraderie that comes with sharing a hearty meal with strangers who quickly become friends.

As you enjoy your beer and bratwurst, the sound of Bavarian music will ll the air. Traditional bands, dressed in lederhosen and dirndls, play lively tunes that will have you're clapping, swaying, and even dancing along. The infectious energy of the music is sure to put a smile on your face and create memories that will last a lifetime.

Oktoberfest is not just about beer, food, and music though. It's also an opportunity to experience the warm and welcoming Bavarian hospitality. Locals and visitors alike come together to celebrate, forming a diverse and inclusive community. Whether you're a solo traveler or part of a group, you'll find that Oktoberfest is a place where everyone is welcome and encouraged to join in the fun.

So, if you're planning a trip to Germany, make sure to include Oktoberfest in Munich on your itinerary. It's a one-of-a-kind experience that combines the best of German beer, bratwurst, and Bavarian music. Whether you're a beer enthusiast, a lover of cultural festivals, or simply looking to immerse yourself in a vibrant atmosphere, Oktoberfest is the perfect destination for you. Prost!

Nuremberg Christmas Markets: Glühwein and Gingerbread

Nuremberg, a city in Bavaria, Germany, is renowned for its charming Christmas markets that attract thousands of visitors each year. The Nuremberg Christmas Markets offer a magical and festive atmosphere, filled with the aromas of mulled wine, roasted almonds, and freshly baked gingerbread. This subchapter explores the enchanting world of Nuremberg's Christmas markets and why they are a must-visit destination for any tourist or traveler.

The Nuremberg Christmas Markets, or Christkindlesmarkt, date back to the 16th century and are steeped in tradition. The market is located in the heart of Nuremberg's old town and features over 180 stalls adorned with twinkling lights and festive decorations. Visitors can browse through an array of handicrafts, Christmas ornaments, and unique gifts, making it the perfect place to find that special souvenir.

One of the highlights of the Nuremberg Christmas Markets is the traditional German holiday drink, Glühwein. This warm, spiced wine is served in decorative mugs and is the perfect way to ward off the winter chill as you explore the market. Sipping on Glühwein while strolling through the stalls is a quintessential Christmas market experience.

Another treat not to be missed at the Nuremberg Christmas Markets is the famous Nuremberg gingerbread, or Lebkuchen. These delicious, soft gingerbread cookies are baked with a blend of spices, honey, and nuts, giving them a unique and irresistible flavor. The aroma of freshly baked Lebkuchen fills the air, creating an inviting and festive atmosphere.

In addition to shopping and indulging in culinary delights, the Nuremberg Christmas Markets offer a variety of entertainment for visitors of all ages. From carol singing and live performances to a children's carousel and an enchanting nativity scene, there is something to captivate everyone's interest.

The Nuremberg Christmas Markets truly embody the spirit of the holiday season and provide an unforgettable experience for tourists and travelers. The combination of festive decorations, delicious treats, and traditional German hospitality make this market a must-visit destination during the Christmas season. Whether you are searching for unique gifts, craving traditional German cuisine, or simply want to immerse yourself in the holiday spirit, the Nuremberg Christmas Markets are sure to leave a lasting impression.

Berlin International Film Festival: Celebrating Cinema and the Arts

The Berlin International Film Festival, also known as the Berlinale, is one of the world's most prestigious and celebrated film festivals. Held annually in the vibrant city of Berlin, this event attracts filmmakers, actors, and cinema enthusiasts from around the globe. With its rich history and commitment to showcasing diverse and groundbreaking films, the Berlinale offers a unique and immersive experience for both tourists and travelers.

The festival was first held in 1951 and has since grown into a renowned platform for international film talent. It takes place in February, turning Berlin into a hub of cinematic excitement. The Berlinale presents a wide range of films, including feature films, documentaries, and short films, from various genres and countries. It serves as a platform for emerging filmmakers as well as established directors, bringing together both established and emerging talent in the industry.

One of the highlights of the Berlinale is the prestigious Golden Bear award, which recognizes outstanding achievements in filmmaking. The award is presented to the best film selected by a jury of industry professionals. The festival also includes other awards such as the Silver Bear for Best Director, Best Actor, and Best Actress, among others.

In addition to film screenings, the Berlinale offers a variety of special events and activities. Visitors can attend panel discussions, workshops, and exhibitions, providing a deeper understanding of the film industry and its creative process. The festival also hosts red carpet premieres, where attendees can catch a glimpse of their favorite actors and filmmakers.

The Berlinale is not only a celebration of cinema but also a reflection of Berlin's vibrant arts scene. The festival takes place in various venues across the city, including the iconic Berlinale Palast in Potsdamer Platz. This central location allows visitors to explore the city's vibrant atmosphere and cultural offerings while attending the festival.

For film enthusiasts and travelers alike, the Berlin International Film Festival offers a unique opportunity to experience the magic of cinema and immerse themselves in the rich arts culture of Berlin. Whether you are a casual moviegoer or a dedicated film buff, the Berlinale is an event not to be missed. Plan your visit during the festival and be a part of this celebration of cinema and the arts in one of the most dynamic cities in the world.

Chapter 8: UNESCO World Heritage Sites: Explore Germany's Architectural and Natural Wonders

Cologne Cathedral: A Gothic Masterpiece

In the heart of the vibrant city of Cologne stands a towering testament to German architectural brilliance - the Cologne Cathedral. This magni cent Gothic masterpiece is not only one of Germany's most iconic landmarks but also a symbol of the country's rich cultural and historical heritage.

The Cologne Cathedral, also known as Kölner Dom, is the epitome of Gothic architecture. Its soaring spires, intricate stone carvings, and stunning stained glass windows make it a sight to behold. As you approach the cathedral, you will be awestruck by its sheer size and grandeur, standing tall at an impressive 157 meters. It is no wonder that the Cologne Cathedral is one of the tallest cathedrals in the world.

Stepping inside this architectural marvel, you will be transported to a world of divine beauty. The interior is adorned with exquisite artworks, including the Shrine of the Three Kings, which is said to contain the remains of the biblical Magi. The intricate details of the cathedral's design, from the ribbed vaults to the ornate altars, will leave you mesmerized.

The history of the Cologne Cathedral is as fascinating as its architecture. Construction of the cathedral began in 1248 but was not completed until 1880, spanning over six centuries. Despite being heavily damaged during World War II, the cathedral was meticulously restored to its former glory, a testament to the resilience and determination of the German people.

Visiting the Cologne Cathedral is an experience that should not be missed when exploring Germany. Whether you are an architecture enthusiast, a history buff, or simply a curious traveler, this Gothic masterpiece will captivate you. Take a guided tour to learn more about the cathedral's fascinating history and the stories behind its magnificent artworks.

As you explore Germany's industrial heritage, make sure to add the Cologne Cathedral to your itinerary. Its historical significance and architectural splendor make it a must-visit destination for tourists and travelers alike. Marvel at the Gothic beauty, soak in the rich history, and be inspired by the masterpiece that is the Cologne Cathedral.

Würzburg Residence: Baroque Splendor and Gardens

The Würzburg Residence is an architectural masterpiece that perfectly exempli es the grandeur and opulence of the Baroque era. Located in the city of Würzburg, in the Franconia region of Germany, this magni cent palace is a must-visit for any tourist or traveler looking to delve into the country's rich history and architectural heritage.

Built in the 18th century for the Prince-Bishops of Würzburg, the Würzburg Residence is a symbol of power and wealth. Designed by the renowned architect Balthasar Neumann, the palace showcases intricate detailing, lavish decorations, and stunning frescoes that will leave visitors in awe. The highlight of the residence is the grand staircase, a masterpiece of Baroque architecture that is considered one of the most beautiful in the world.

The palace is also home to an extensive art collection, featuring works by famous artists such as Tiepolo and G.B. Tiepolo. From the opulent Imperial Hall to the exquisite Mirror Cabinet, each room is a testament to the artistic and cultural significance of the era.

Beyond the palace itself, the Würzburg Residence is surrounded by breathtaking gardens that add to its allure. The Court Garden, with its meticulously manicured lawns, fountains, and statues, offers a peaceful retreat for visitors to wander and admire the beauty of nature. The Palace Garden, on the other hand, is a haven of tranquility, featuring terraces, flower beds, and a vineyard that produces the renowned Würzburg wine.

Visiting the Würzburg Residence is not only an opportunity to appreciate architectural splendor, but also to learn about the history of Germany. The palace has witnessed significant events, including the meeting of the Congress of Vienna in 1814, making it a site of historical importance.

For tourists and travelers seeking a unique and enriching experience in Germany, the Würzburg Residence is a must-see destination. Its stunning architecture, awe-inspiring interiors, and picturesque gardens make it one of the top 15 places to visit in the country. Whether you are interested in history, art, or simply want to bask in the beauty of the Baroque era, a visit to the Würzburg Residence will leave you with unforgettable memories and a deeper appreciation for Germany's cultural heritage.

Upper Middle Rhine Valley: Castles and Romantic Landscapes

The Upper Middle Rhine Valley: Castles and Romantic Landscapes

The Upper Middle Rhine Valley is a picturesque region in Germany that is renowned for its stunning castles and romantic landscapes. This subchapter will take you on a journey through this enchanting area, highlighting its rich history and breathtaking views.

As you explore the Upper Middle Rhine Valley, you will be captivated by its fairytale-like castles that are perched atop hills overlooking the serene Rhine River. These castles, such as Marksburg Castle and Rheinfels Castle, have stood the test of time and offer a glimpse into Germany's medieval past. Their towering turrets and stone walls create a sense of awe and wonder, making them must-visit destinations for any tourist or traveler.

Beyond the castles, the Upper Middle Rhine Valley is also known for its romantic landscapes. The rolling hills, vineyards, and quaint villages create a postcard-perfect setting that will transport you back in time. Take a leisurely stroll through the charming village of Bacharach, with its half-timbered houses and cobblestone streets, or embark on a scenic boat cruise along the Rhine River to fully appreciate the beauty of this region.

In addition to its natural beauty, the Upper Middle Rhine Valley is steeped in history. It has been recognized as a UNESCO World Heritage Site due to its exceptional cultural landscape and architectural treasures. The region's castles, vineyards, and charming towns all contribute to its unique character and historical significance.

For wine enthusiasts, the Upper Middle Rhine Valley is a paradise. The region is famous for its vineyards that produce some of the finest Riesling wines in the world. A visit to the picturesque town of Rüdesheim will allow you to indulge in wine tastings and explore the vineyards that line the hillsides.

The Upper Middle Rhine Valley truly offers a magical experience for tourists and travelers. Whether you are drawn to its fairytale castles, romantic landscapes, or rich history, this region will leave you with lasting memories. Immerse yourself in the beauty and charm of the Upper Middle Rhine Valley, and discover why it is considered one of Germany's top 15 places to visit.

Aachen Cathedral: Charlemagne's Palatine Chapel

One of the most historically significant sites in Germany, Aachen Cathedral, also known as the Imperial Cathedral of Aachen, it is a must-visit destination for any tourist or traveler seeking to explore the rich history of the country. This iconic cathedral holds a special place in German history as the Palatine Chapel of Emperor Charlemagne, making it a fascinating site to explore.

Located in the picturesque city of Aachen in western Germany, the cathedral showcases a unique blend of architectural styles, reflecting the various periods of its construction over the centuries. From its early Romanesque elements to the Gothic additions, the cathedral stands as a testament to the rich architectural heritage of Germany.

A highlight of the Aachen Cathedral is the Palatine Chapel, which was built by Charlemagne in the 8th century. This magnificent structure features intricate mosaics, stunning marble columns, and a golden mosaic ceiling that depicts biblical scenes. Stepping into the chapel is like stepping back in time, as visitors can experience the grandeur and splendor that once surrounded the great Emperor Charlemagne.

Aside from its historical significance, Aachen Cathedral is also a place of pilgrimage for many devout Christians. The cathedral houses the relics of Charlemagne, making it an important religious site. Visitors can pay their respects to the great Emperor and immerse themselves in the spiritual atmosphere of this holy place.

In addition to the Palatine Chapel, the cathedral complex boasts other architectural gems, such as the Gothic choir and the Ottonian westwork. Exploring these different sections of the cathedral allows visitors to appreciate the evolution of German architecture and the influence of different artistic styles throughout history.

A visit to Aachen Cathedral is an opportunity to delve into the depths of Germany's past and witness the grandeur of one of Europe's most important historical figures, Charlemagne. Whether you are a history enthusiast, an architecture lover, or simply a traveler seeking to immerse yourself in the cultural heritage of Germany, Aachen Cathedral is a destination not to be missed.

Chapter 9: Industrial Heritage: Discover Germany's Industrial Past

Zollverein Coal Mine Industrial Complex: From Coal Mines to Cultural Center

The Zollverein Coal Mine Industrial Complex in Essen, Germany, is a remarkable testament to the country's industrial history and a must-visit destination for tourists and travelers seeking a unique cultural experience. This subchapter will delve into the transformation of this former coal mining site into a vibrant cultural center that offers a fascinating blend of history, architecture, and contemporary art.

The Zollverein Coal Mine, a UNESCO World Heritage Site, was once one of the largest and most productive coal mines in Europe. It played a crucial role in Germany's industrial development and served as the backbone of the nation's economy for decades. However, as the demand for coal declined, the mine closed its doors in 1986, leaving behind a massive industrial complex that seemed destined for abandonment.

Fortunately, visionary architects and cultural enthusiasts recognized the potential of this industrial monument and embarked on a journey to transform it into a vibrant cultural hub. Today, the Zollverein Coal Mine Industrial Complex stands as an architectural masterpiece, blending the historic structures of the old mine with contemporary design elements.

Visitors to the complex can explore the former mine buildings, including the iconic coal washing plant, which now houses a museum showcasing the history of coal mining in the region. The museum offers a captivating journey through time, with interactive exhibits, multimedia presentations, and preserved mining machinery that provide insight into the lives of the miners who toiled in these underground tunnels.

Beyond the museum, the Zollverein Coal Mine Industrial Complex is also home to a range of cultural institutions, including theaters, galleries, and exhibition spaces. Art lovers can admire contemporary artworks by renowned artists, while theater enthusiasts can catch captivating performances that explore the intersection of art, culture and industry.

For those seeking culinary delights, the complex boasts several restaurants and cafes that serve delicious regional cuisine. Visitors can savor traditional dishes made from locally sourced ingredients while enjoying the unique atmosphere of this transformed industrial site.

In conclusion, the Zollverein Coal Mine Industrial Complex is a remarkable testament to Germany's industrial heritage. Its transformation from a coal mine to a thriving cultural center is a shining example of how historical sites can be repurposed to create vibrant spaces that celebrate both the past and the present. A visit to this site will undoubtedly leave tourists and travelers with a deep appreciation for Germany's rich industrial history and its commitment to preserving and repurposing its heritage for future generations.

Speicherstadt Warehouse District: A Symbol of Hamburg's Trading History

The Speicherstadt Warehouse District: A Symbol of Hamburg's Trading History

The Speicherstadt Warehouse District in Hamburg is not only a remarkable sight to behold but also a testament to the city's rich trading history. This subchapter will explore the significance of this industrial heritage site, making it one of the top 15 places to visit in Germany for tourists and travelers seeking a unique and historical experience.

Situated between the Elbe River and the city center, the Speicherstadt Warehouse District is the largest warehouse district in the world. Built in the late 19th century, it was originally designed to store valuable goods such as spices, coffee, tea, and carpets. The district's red-brick buildings, intricate architecture, and network of canals create a truly picturesque and atmospheric setting.

As visitors stroll through the labyrinthine streets, they will be transported back in time to an era when Hamburg was a thriving trading hub. The district's warehouses, with their characteristic gabled roofs and ornate facades, evoke a sense of grandeur and prestige. Inside, some of these warehouses have been transformed into museums, showcasing artifacts and exhibits that tell the story of Hamburg's maritime and trading past.

One of the highlights of the Speicherstadt Warehouse District is the Miniatur Wunderland, the world's largest model railway. Covering an area of over 1,500 square meters, this intricate display features detailed replicas of famous landmarks, bustling cities, and picturesque landscapes from around the world, providing visitors with a mesmerizing and immersive experience.

For those interested in the inner workings of the district, a boat tour along the canals is a must. As the boat glides through the waterways, visitors can marvel at the impressive architecture and gain a deeper understanding of the district's importance in facilitating global trade.

Moreover, the Speicherstadt Warehouse District is not just a historical site but a vibrant cultural hub. It is home to numerous art galleries, theaters, and trendy cafes, making it a popular destination for locals and tourists alike.

In conclusion, the Speicherstadt Warehouse District in Hamburg offers a unique and immersive experience that allows visitors to delve into the city's trading history. From its stunning architecture to its fascinating museums and cultural offerings, this industrial heritage site is a must-visit for anyone seeking a glimpse into Germany's rich past.

Völklingen Ironworks: A UNESCO World Heritage Site

Germany is known for its rich history and diverse cultural heritage, and one place that perfectly encapsulates this is the Völklingen Ironworks. Located in the Saarland region, this industrial marvel has been designated as a UNESCO World Heritage Site, and for good reason.

The Völklingen Ironworks stands as a testament to Germany's industrial past, showcasing the country's significant contribution to the iron and steel industry. Built in the late 19th century, this massive ironworks complex played a crucial role in Germany's industrial revolution. At its height, it was one of the largest ironworks in Europe, employing thousands of workers and producing millions of tons of iron and steel.

Today, the Völklingen Ironworks has been transformed into a captivating museum and cultural center, allowing visitors to step back in time and experience the industrial heritage of Germany. As you explore the sprawling complex, you'll be immersed in the sights, sounds, and stories of the workers who toiled here. From the towering blast furnaces to the intricate machinery, every corner of the ironworks offers a glimpse into the past.

One of the highlights of the Völklingen Ironworks is the stunning exhibition spaces that have been created within the industrial setting. These spaces host a variety of rotating exhibits, showcasing contemporary art, photography, and installations that reflect the ironworks' history and significance. It's a unique blend of the old and the new, creating a truly immersive experience for visitors.

Beyond the museum, the Völklingen Ironworks also hosts cultural events and concerts, adding to its vibrant atmosphere. From live music performances to theater productions, there's always something happening at this dynamic World Heritage Site.

For tourists and travelers seeking a deeper understanding of Germany's industrial past, the Völklingen Ironworks is a must-visit destination. Its inclusion on the list of top 15 places to visit in Germany is well-deserved, as it offers a unique and educational experience unlike any other. So, whether you're a history enthusiast or simply curious about Germany's industrial heritage, make sure to add the Völklingen Ironworks to your itinerary. It's a journey through time that you won't soon forget.

Chapter 10: Natural Landscapes: Experience Germany's Diverse Natural Beauty

Black Forest: Dense Forests and Cuckoo Clocks

Nestled in the southwestern region of Germany lies the captivating Black Forest, a destination that combines dense forests with the charm of traditional cuckoo clocks. This subchapter takes you on a journey through this enchanting region, highlighting its natural beauty and cultural significance.

The Black Forest, or Schwarzwald in German, gets its name from the thick canopy of evergreen trees that cover its landscape. As you venture into this mystical forest, you'll find yourself surrounded by towering trees, winding trails, and an abundance of wildlife. Whether you're an avid hiker, nature lover, or simply seeking tranquility, the Black Forest offers an idyllic retreat away from the bustling cities.

One of the most iconic symbols of the Black Forest is the cuckoo clock. Stepping into a traditional Black Forest village, you'll be greeted by the melodic sounds of these intricately crafted timepieces. These clocks have a rich history dating back to the 18th century and are handcrafted with precision and care. Visiting a cuckoo clock workshop allows you to witness the skill and artistry that goes into creating these timeless treasures.

Beyond its natural beauty and cuckoo clocks, the Black Forest is also renowned for its culinary delights. Indulge in the region's famous Black Forest cake, a decadent dessert made with layers of chocolate cake, cherries, and whipped cream. You can also savor the flavors of local delicacies such as Black Forest ham, smoked sausages, and hearty stews.

For outdoor enthusiasts, the Black Forest offers a myriad of activities. Lace up your hiking boots and explore the vast network of hiking trails that crisscross the region. From leisurely strolls to challenging treks, there's a trail for every level of adventurer. You can also cycle along scenic routes, paddle across pristine lakes, or even try your hand at skiing during the winter months.

In addition to its natural wonders, the Black Forest is dotted with charming towns and villages that exude a fairytale-like atmosphere. Wander through the narrow cobblestone streets of towns like Triberg or Freiburg, admiring the half-timbered houses and oral displays. Don't miss the opportunity to visit the Black Forest Open Air Museum, where you can step back in time and learn about the region's rural traditions and customs.

Whether you're captivated by the allure of dense forests, fascinated by the craftsmanship of cuckoo clocks, or simply seeking a peaceful escape, the Black Forest promises an unforgettable experience. Immerse yourself in the beauty and charm of this region, and you'll leave with lasting memories of Germany's natural and cultural heritage.

10.

10. Industrial Heritage: Discover Germany's Industrial Past

Germany's rich and diverse history extends far beyond its fairy tale castles and romantic villages. For those with a fascination for the industrial revolution and the development of modern infrastructure, Germany offers a unique opportunity to explore its industrial heritage. From coal mines to warehouses, these sites provide a glimpse into the country's industrial past and the impact it has had on its present.

One must-visit site is the Zollverein Coal Mine Industrial Complex in Essen. Once one of the largest coal mines in the world, this UNESCO World Heritage Site has been transformed into a cultural center, showcasing the country's industrial history. Explore the former mine shafts, visit the impressive coking plant, and learn about the lives of the miners who toiled underground.

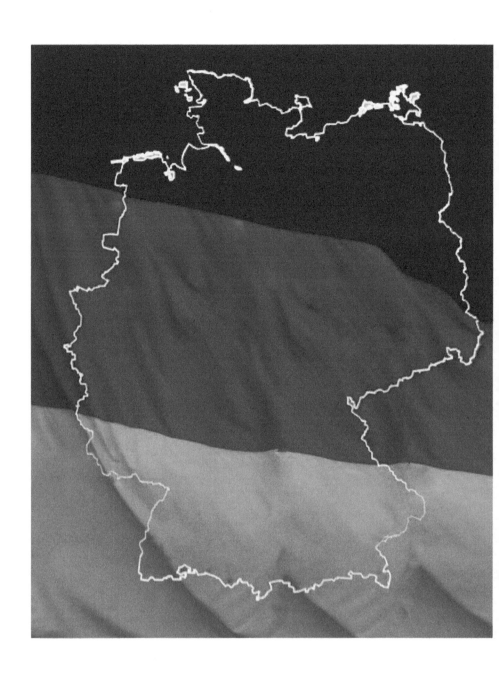

Another remarkable industrial site is the Speicherstadt warehouse district in Hamburg. Built in the late 19th century, this complex of red-brick buildings is the largest warehouse district in the world. Take a stroll along the canals and admire the architectural beauty of the warehouses, which once served as storage for goods from all over the world. Today, many of these buildings have been repurposed into museums, cafes, and shops, creating a vibrant atmosphere in this historic district.

Visiting Germany's industrial heritage sites not only provides an understanding of the country's past but also highlights its commitment to preserving and repurposing these sites for the future. These locations offer unique insights into the technological advancements that shaped Germany's growth as an industrial powerhouse.

Whether you are a history enthusiast or simply curious about the development of modern infrastructure, exploring Germany's industrial heritage is an experience that should not be missed. Immerse yourself in the stories of the miners, factory workers, and merchants who played a crucial role in shaping Germany's industrial landscape. From the Zollverein Coal Mine Industrial Complex to the Speicherstadt warehouse district, these sites offer a fascinating journey through time and provide a deeper appreciation for the country's industrial legacy.

So, when planning your trip to Germany, don't forget to include these industrial heritage sites in your itinerary. They are not only historically signi cant but also offer a unique perspective on the country's industrial prowess and the resilience of its people. Experience the transformation of coal mines into cultural centers and warehouses into vibrant districts, and gain a deeper understanding of Germany's industrial past.

Abdurahmane Diallo

Augsburg Germany

Made in the USA
Las Vegas, NV
15 February 2024

85833631R00125